Problems cannot be solved at the same level of awareness
that created them.

—Albert Einstein

Getting Steamed to Overcome Corporatism

Build It Together to Win

Ralph Nader

common courage press
monroe, maine

ISBN (paper): 978-1-56751-406-3
ISBN ebook: 978-1-56751-407-0

Library of Congress Cataloging-in-Publication Data
Nader, Ralph.
Getting steamed : to overcome corporatism, build it together to win / Ralph Nader.
p. cm.
Includes index.
ISBN 978-1-56751-406-3 (pbk. : alk. paper) -- ISBN 978-1-56751-407-0 (ebk.)
1. Corporate state. I. Title.

JC478.N33 2011
322'.30973--dc23

2011032453

Common Courage Press
P.O. Box 702
121 Red Barn Road
Monroe, ME 04951

207-525-0900
fax: 207-525-3068

www.commoncouragepress.com
info@commoncouragepress.com

SECOND PRINTING

Dedication

To all Americans who get steamed enough to join together in action,
as urged in the aftermath of this book.

Contents

Introduction
Getting Ready for the Experiment

This is an invitation to participate in an experiment to learn what, if anything, it takes to get you steamed* for action for a change.

Let's start with a simple question. When you read about an injustice by a corporation against a patient, consumer, worker, taxpayer, or community, do you, like most people, recoil with dismay or disgust and then return to your workaday world? If that's your reaction, is it because you do not have the *power* to do anything about it, don't *know* how to do anything about it, don't have the *time* to do anything about it or all of the above?

What do you think would happen to how you answer these questions if you read one after another about ten, twenty, one hundred or two hundred corporate abuses, harms and crimes, especially if you start saying, "This happened to my neighbor" or "my friend" or "my children" or "my co-worker" or "This could easily happen to me"?

Well, plunge into the following engrossing pages reporting the virulent misbehavior of big business in the pursuit of grotesque profits. The actions of these corporate outlaws are documented by mainstream media and well-regarded specialized publications. Even when these greedy over-reaching bullies are sometimes caught, the punishment is usually too little and too late. Moreover, their invidious practices often continue through other domestic or international companies in the same industry.

The *aggregation* of these outrages—all reported in just one year—2009—can spark your conscience and stiffen your resolve to speak out with other Americans or support much greater

---

*Steam generates the power to turn the turbines that produce electricity—the major "enlightenment" of applied physics.

reforms and law enforcement against corporate crime. Or at least that is this experiment's hypothesis. Each story helps you to recalibrate what is important to talk about with your friends, to think about and to challenge.

After all, the Wall Street orgy of crime, speculation, recklessness and self-enrichment looted or drained trillions of dollars from pensions and mutual funds, drove the country into a deep recession in 2009 that unemployed over 8 million workers. The repercussions continue to this day in insecurity, debt, deprivation, rising poverty, fifty million uninsured, and Wal-Mart-level wages for one out of three workers in the declining economy. Yet corporate profits hit record levels in 2010. Executive compensation for the corporate bosses has resumed its grotesque disparity with working Americans. Corporate lobbyists still dominate "our" federal government that bailed out the out-of-control companies big-time with your taxpayer money. There have been no apologies, no expressions of shame, just business as usual heading toward another climax of greed and abandon that will fall again on the taxpayers' back. Cutbacks for necessities of the American people come before cutbacks for corporate welfare, while a bloated, corrupt military budget continues to nourish insatiable weapons contractors. A commercial culture runs roughshod over civic values and parental authority to expose their children to a 24/7 world of gross, often violent entertainment, harmful products and junk food.

Our country, our culture, our democratic heritage are all in decay, with no end in sight unless there is a sustained response from an aroused citizenry to stop the corporatists from blocking so many proven solutions for our country's problems. First, we need to raise our *expectations* to realistically attainable levels so we can believe that a better country is possible soon.

Back in the 1950's I, like many others in that era, lost several friends and classmates to motor vehicle crashes—horrific fatalities and injuries. At law school, I learned the truth about the auto industry bosses, who, in favor of styling priorities, restrained their safety engineers and scientists from installing long-known safety devices like seat belts, better brakes and tires, collapsible steering columns and interior padding. And, *I got steamed*. With the tragedy of so many people in preventable crashes and casualties always on my mind, I pressed the Congress month after month to pass the 1966 motor vehicle and highway safety laws, which have saved over a million lives and prevented many more injuries. What drove me and inspired my commitment was not just my knowledge of the industry's cover-up, but an ample amount of informed indignation (the psychologists now call this 'emotional intelligence') and the best from America's past.

Throughout our history, enough Americans finally became steamed against slavery, for women's right to vote, for better treatment of workers and farmers, for protection of consumers and the environment. That's when conditions started changing for the better.

Did you ever see that movie NETWORK in which the leading actor got fed up enough to shout to all who would listen "I'M AS MAD AS HELL AND I'M NOT GOING TO TAKE IT ANYMORE?" The two times I saw this film in a movie theatre, the audience clapped vigorously after this line. Such is the built-up power of moral indignation conveyed to the viewers by the escalating frustration he was absorbing.

To get the full impact, don't put this book down. Give yourself a chance to alter your mental routines and focus your energies. Read these jolting or jarring excerpts and comments through in as few sittings as possible.

After you finish, you may want to explore joining with others of like mind and sensibility for action that makes these big corporations (all brought into existence by state charters) our servants, not our masters. After all that is what is implied in our constitution's preamble "We the People" (it's *not* We the corporation) and implied in the free market's slogan that "the customer is always right." Thank you for taking this "test."

See you in a few hours in the Aftermath section!!

—Ralph Nader

GETTING STEAMED!!

CORPORATE OUTRAGES

[According to a recent study,] "[T]he uninsured have a higher risk of death when compared to the privately insured, even after taking into account socioeconomics, health behaviors and baseline health," said lead author Dr. Andrew Wilper ("Health Insurance and Mortality in U.S. Adults." *American Journal of Public Health*, December 2009).

"Historically, every other developed nation has achieved universal healthcare through some form of nonprofit national health insurance," said study co-author Dr. Steffie Woolhandler, a professor of medicine at Harvard and a primary care physician in Cambridge, Massachusetts. "Our failure to do so means that all Americans pay higher health care costs, and 45,000 pay with their lives." Even the whittled down version of the Senate bill would leave 25 million uninsured. That translates into about 25,000 deaths annually from lack of health insurance.

"Absent the $400 billion in savings you could get from single payer, universal coverage is unaffordable. Politicians in Washington are protecting insurance profits while sacrificing American lives."

"Now one American dies every 12 minutes," said study co-author Dr. David Himmelstein.

"California leads the nation with 5,302 deaths due to lack of health insurance per year. Texas follows closely behind with 4,675 deaths due to lack of health insurance per year. Texas also had the highest rate (in 2005) of uninsured citizens—29.7 percent."

Source: *Corporate Crime Reporter*, September 21, 2009

Comment: Since President Theodore Roosevelt urged universal health insurance about 100 years ago, the medical-drug-insurance-corporate complex has blocked this life-saving coverage for the American people. No other Western country lets its people die, stay sick or injured for lack of health insurance.

* * *

The health insurance companies, such as Aetna, Cigna and United HealthCare, make more money by denying claims and benefits, and by excluding tens of millions of Americans. Among these people are an estimated 2,266 U.S. military veterans under the age of 65 who died in 2009 "because they lacked health insurance and thus had reduced access to care. At this rate since the 2003 invasion in Iraq about three times more of these uninsured veterans have lost their lives than the combined U.S. soldiers' fatalities in Iraq and Afghanistan." (According to Harvard Medical school researcher Dr. David Himmelstein, the co-author of an analysis [of health insurance]). "Like other uninsured Americans, most uninsured vets are working people—too poor to afford private coverage, but not poor enough to qualify for Medicaid or means-tested VA care," said Dr. Steffie Woolhandler, a professor at Harvard Medical School.

Source: *Public Citizen Health Letter*, December 2009

Nine scientists within the Food and Drug Administration (FDA), in a letter to then president-elect Barack Obama and to Congress, describe a corrupt review process in which medical devices are given quick approval following perfunctory testing because manufacturers tell the FDA that their products are "me too" devices that operate similarly as older devices that have already received agency approval. Subsequently, the FDA scientists pointed out "imaging equipment to detect breast cancer and an orthopedic knee device that had been inappropriately approved by the agency" as examples. A Government Accountability Office (GAO) report made similar criticisms of the FDA for "failing to protect the public by its lax or minimal testing of medical devices."

Source: *Public Citizen Health Letter,* December 2009

Comment: The medical device industry, with sales of approximately $336 billion in 2008, is a powerful lobby in Washington, D.C. Even Senator Al Franken took the industry's side in an Obama proposal to lightly tax them to help pay for the health insurance law.

* * *

Not so long ago, women of a certain age in the U.S. were made to believe that going on hormonal replacement therapy (HRT) was as much of a rite of passage as menarche or pregnancy. Over the past seven years, however, we have learned just how wrong that was: the science on which the prescription was based was flawed, the data were consistently misinterpreted, and the medical literature on which medical practices was based was on a very shaky foundation. This whole edifice fell apart in 2002, when a large federally funded study stopped after finding that menopausal women who took certain hormones had an increased risk of invasive breast cancer, heart disease and stroke.

Now, we know that the rise of HRT cannot be attributed to well-meaning but misguided scientists, but rather to out-and-out fraud. Wyeth, manufacturer of Premarin and Prempro, contracted with a medical communication firm to write articles favorable to its products, and then paid (until then) reputable doctors to appear as authors. The articles were published in 18 established medical journals such as *The American Journal of Obstetrics and Gynecology*, and the *International Journal of Cardiology*. These articles in effect gave the imprimatur to practices which then spread widely. And the medical literature in turn spawned a variety of more popular "chick lit" articles and books with enticing titles that touted the benefits of being "forever feminine"while avoiding dry skin and a diminished libido. The result? Millions of women were duped while Wyeth sold $2 billion worth of drugs in 2001 alone.

Source: *Public Citizen Health Letter*, September 2009

The $2.3 billion settlement between Pfizer and the U.S. Justice Department for unlawful prescription drug promotion may sound large, but it's not enough to ensure drug companies will curb their bad behavior.

That's the take of Dr. Sidney Wolfe of Public Citizen's Health

Research Group.

Pfizer has broken a record just set by Eli Lilly & Company in January for what was then described by the Justice Department as the largest individual corporate criminal fine in U.S. history—more than $500 million in criminal penalties for off-label promotion of Zyprexa. Now, a scant seven months later, Pfizer has broken this record with a criminal fine of $1.2 billion, the largest criminal fine ever imposed in the U.S. for any matter.

"The U.S. pharmaceutical industry, long one of the most profitable in the country, with profits last year of close to $50 billion, has engaged in an unprecedented amount of criminal activity in the past decade, all aimed at increasing sales, often by illegally promoting drugs for diseases for which evidence that benefits outweigh harm is lacking," Wolfe said. "When doctors are induced, either by being bribed or misled by drug companies, to prescribe drugs for such purposes, there is a reasonable chance that the drugs will do more harm than good and patients may be seriously injured or killed by such promotion."

Pfizer also pled guilty to criminal charges for off-label promotion of Neurontin in 2004.

In addition to Pfizer and Eli Lilly, other companies have been found to have engaged in criminal activity in the past 10 years include Abbott, Schering-Plough, AstraZeneca, Perdue and Bayer.

"It is not surprising," Wolfe said, "that the American public understands this. In a Harris Poll last fall, only ten percent of respondents thought that the pharmaceutical industry was 'generally honest and trustworthy—so that you normally believe a statement by a company in that industry.'

"Until corporate titans are forced to fork over a much larger proportion of their illegally gotten profits and are put behind bars, nothing will change," Wolfe said.

Source: *Corporate Crime Reporter*, September 7, 2009

More than 22 years after the federal government started tracking serious disciplinary actions against non-physician health workers, the infractions—everything from fraud and abuse to improperly prescribing drugs—are still kept secret from most hospitals and many nursing homes doing background checks of potential employees.

The Healthcare Integrity and Protection Data Bank contains discipline records for more than 100,000 nurses, physician assistants, pharmacists and other non-physician health workers.

"Many of these workers would not have jobs in the health care field if their current employers knew about their checkered pasts," said Dr. Sidney Wolfe, M.D., director of Public Citizen's Health Research Group. "Keeping these records secret greatly increases the chance that patients will be injured or killed at the hands of their caretakers."

Source: *Public Citizen Health Letter*, September 2009

Comment: A similar situation prevails with questionable doctors. Since 1986, federal law requires that hospitals report to the National Practitioners Data Bank (NPDB) whenever they revoke or restrict a physician's hospital privileges for more than 30 days for problems involving medical competency or conduct. As of December 2007, almost 50 percent of the hospitals in the U.S. had never reported a single privilege sanction to the NPDB. Prior to the opening of the NPDB in September 1990, the federal government estimated that 5,000 hospital clinical privilege reports would be submitted to the NPDB on an annual basis, while the health care industry estimated 10,000 reports per year. However, the average number of annual reports has been only 650 for the 17 years of the NPDB's existence, which is one-eighth of the government estimate and about one-sixteenth of the industry estimate.

See the *Health Letter* (citizen.org/hrgpublications), July 2009, for a specific outrageous example of criminal medical practice on patients, and *Health Letter*, May 2009, for a report on psycho-prostitution.

* * *

It's been one of the oldest and most widely prescribed painkillers but it may soon be taken off the market. The drug in question? Propoxyphene, known by the brand names Darvon and, when combined with acetaminophen, Darvocet. Dr. Sidney Wolfe has urged withdrawal of the dangerous drugs for 30 years. "In 2007, it was the 21st most-prescribed generic drug, with 21.3 million prescriptions written that year," [he said].

"For far less money, patients would get more pain relief if they took aspirin or acetaminophen," Dr. Wolfe has testified.

"It provides about the same relief as aspirin, and 'in excessive doses, either alone or in combination with other (central nervous system) depressants, including alcohol, is a major cause of drug related deaths,' according to the 'black box' warning that the FDA currently requires manufacturers to include in the labeling" [he added]. On January 30, 2009, two Food and Drug Administration (FDA) advisory committees recommended that the FDA should pull propoxyphene, Darvon and Darvocet from the market. Thousands of people have died while the FDA feared taking on the involved drug companies.

Source: *Public Citizen News*, March/April 2009

* * *

Comment: On November 19, 2010 Dr. Sidney Wolfe, Director, Public Citizen's Health Research Group issued a statement on Darvon/Darvocet. Dr. Wolfe said, "The announcement by the U.S. Food and Drug Administration (FDA) that propoxyphene-containing products are finally going to be taken off the market—because of dangers previously known and acted upon, with bans announced in the UK almost six years ago, and in Europe, almost 1☐ years ago—is a serious indictment of the FDA's long-lasting unwillingness to protect people in this country from a deadly but barely effective painkiller."

* * *

The widely prescribed diabetes drug Avandia should be banned immediately because it can cause deadly liver failure in addition to other potentially fatal problems, according to new *Public Citizen* research published in a peer-reviewed medical journal ...The new research adds weight to *Public Citizen*'s October 2008 petition to the FDA to ban Avandia because of its risks of [causing] heart attack, heart failure and liver toxicity...Another diabetes drug, Actos, is known to cause heart failure and increase the risk of fractures. *Public Citizen* lists Actos alongside Avandia as a "do not use" drug on its Web site, worstpills.org.

"Many other, safer drugs than Actos or Avandia are available to treat Type 2 diabetes and do not carry the same risk of liver toxicity."

Source: *Public Citizen News* January/February 2011

Comment: There are about 100,000 Americans who die every year from adverse reactions to the effects of approved, prescription drugs, just a staggering toll year after year! In addition approximately 1.5 million people in the United States are hospitalized annually due to adverse reactions to their medicines. For further information on the kinds of injuries and illnesses, see *Worst Pills, Best Pills* by Dr. Sidney Wolfe, et al. Pocket Books (New York, 2005).

* * *

Tired truckers are a menace to themselves and to others on the highways. In 2009 safety groups petitioned the U.S. Court of Appeals for the District of Columbia to overturn the hours-of-service rule issued by George W. Bush in 2003. The dangerous rule actually increased the number of daily and weekly hours truckers can drive to 11 consecutive hours (instead of 10) each shift, and up to 17 hours more driving (77 hours instead of 60) each week. The rule dramatically expands driving and work hours by cutting the off-duty rest and recovery time at the end of the week from a full weekend of 50 or more hours off duty to as little as only 34 hours off-duty.

Source: *Public Citizen News*, September/October 2009

Comment: The trucking industry lobby is unusually powerful in Washington, D.C. They dominate the position of the regulatory agency (the Federal Motor Carrier Safety Administration) on trucker fatigue, notwithstanding the loss of almost 5,000 lives due to truck crashes every year.

* * *

A newly formed coalition is calling on Congress to stand up for employees and consumers and ensure companies are held accountable for misdeeds by passing legislation to end forced arbitration. The Fair Arbitration Now Coalition's goal is to pass the Arbitration Fairness Act (H.R. 1020). Participants represent consumers, workers, homeowners, franchise holders and more. ... Many industry groups are actively lobbying lawmakers, pressing them to allow businesses to continue what many consider a predatory practice.

Forced arbitration clauses are hidden in the fine print of employment, cell phone, credit card, retirement account, home building, nursing home and assisted living contracts, to name a few. Just by taking a job or buying a product or service, individuals are forced to give up their right to go to court if they are harmed by a company. Because the private system of forced arbitration benefits companies and disadvantages consumers and employees, more and more industries are using the tactic of forced arbitration to evade accountability.

The coalition also has launched a web site, www. FairArbitrationNow.org, explaining what forced arbitration is, outlining the kinds of contracts in which forced arbitration clauses appear, providing links to news articles and telling stories of arbitration horrors.

Source: *Corporate Crime Reporter*, April 27, 2009

Comment: No government can get away with blocking your right to go to court to resolve an injustice against the perpetrator of your harm. But corporations can. They use the fine print to impose compulsory arbitration should there be a dispute between you and your seller. They rig the arbitration process, often do not disclose their arbitration policies, and do not compete over their fine print contracts. So you cannot "go across the street" to a competitor for a better fine print deal whether they be insurance companies, banks, hospitals, auto dealers or the whole bunch of Internet, cable, and telephone corporations. However, progress is being made by persistent consumer groups like Public Citizen. In 2009, the giant Bank of America announced it was quitting the "binding arbitration" requirement in its contracts with customers.

* * *

The corporate welfare freeloaders—nuclear power companies—stepped up their demand for you, the taxpayers, to guarantee their new nukes against default on their Wall Street loans. For years, the big banks have refused to lend electric companies money to build these costly plants without Uncle Sam guaranteeing them against any losses. Corporate socialism on demand. Well, building nukes is risky and they come in about 207 percent higher than their initial cost projection. A May 2003 Congressional Budget Office (CBO) report showed that the risk of default on loan guarantees to build nuclear plants is "very high, well above 50 percent."

After the absence of any firm orders for nuclear plants since the mid-seventies, the pummeled administrations of George W. Bush and Barack Obama have sent to Congress requests to approve nearly $70 billion in loan guarantees administered by the patsy Nuclear Regulatory Commission. Each reactor cost $9 billion to $15 billion to build and, if history repeats itself, four out of seven loans will default.

Source: *Public Citizen News*, November/December 2009

Comment: Renewables and conservation (megawatts) are beating nuclear power all over the world in the free market. They are cheaper, faster to install, safer on the ground and for the climate, and do not present earthquake security, disposal and evacuation nightmares in situ or on highways, bridges and railroads. See "Climate: Eight Convenient Truths," November 9, 2009, in *Roll Call* by Amory Lovins, chairman and chief scientist of the Rocky

Mountain Institute.

* * *

The old Phillip Morris no longer exists. In March, the company formally divided itself into two separate entities: Philip Morris USA, which remains a part of the parent company Altria, and Philip Morris International.

Philip Morris International has already signaled its initial plans to subvert the most important policies to reduce smoking and the toll from tobacco-related disease (now at 5 million lives lost a year). The company has announced plans to inflict on the world an array of new products, packages and marketing efforts. These are designed to undermine smoke-free workplace rules, defeat tobacco taxes, segment markets with specially flavored products, offer flavored cigarettes sure to appeal to youth and overcome marketing restrictions.

Source: *The Progressive Populist*, February 1, 2009

Comment: Year after year the U.S. Surgeon General reports that around 400,000 Americans die annually, more than 1,000 people a day, from diseases related to smoking such as lung cancer. The anti-smoking and non-smoking movements in our country have made great strides in cutting the adult smoking rate by more than half (around 20 percent of adults smoke regularly now) since 1965, and have established through law or persuasion non-smoking areas, starting with passenger aircraft, and interstate trains and buses back in the seventies. The tobacco companies see less developed countries in Asia, Africa and South America as their growth area, especially targeting the young with seductive advertisements. By growth the Western tobacco companies mean sales and profit growth. But they are sure to generate growth in cancer and heart diseases until the rule of law and non-smoker pressures build in these countries.

* * *

The Mortgage Thieves Return. First come the shady operators, then comes the bailout, then come the shady operators. That, too often, is the sad history of financial meltdowns and their cleanups.

The closing days of the Bush administration offer the familiar spectacle of bad actors descending on a government program fat with new money and starved of oversight. The object of plunder this time is a Federal Housing Administration (FHA) program recently empowered to extend an additional $300 billion in loan guarantees, reports *Business Week*.

The plunderers include the seediest of subprime mortgage lenders, back for a second feeding, this time off the taxpayers.

Criminal convictions, bankruptcies, state sanctions and civil lawsuits rarely pose an obstacle to these players. They've changed their spiel, and some have changed their name.

The FHA guidelines endure, but unscrupulous mortgage companies can work around them. They can still use phony data to certify unqualified buyers and inflate the prices of the houses being sold. And they are doing just that. The loss to taxpayers from new FHA loans could exceed $100 billion over the next five years, predicts an industry newsletter, *Inside Mortgage Finance*.

Source: *The Progressive Populist*, February 1, 2009 (by Froma Harrop)

Comment: Exacerbating the crimes is the fact that FHA's staff monitoring the lenders and approving new ones totals five people to cover more than 36,000 FHA-authorized lenders.

* * *

Every day shoppers go into stores, buy necessities and pay anywhere from five to eight percent sales tax, depending on the state. Day after day investors in speculative derivatives turn over two or three trillion dollars in such transactions and pay no sales tax.

Wall Street has blocked any such "transaction tax" even though numerous industrialized countries like the UK and Japan collect it. Congress whimpers. Wall Street escapes, laughing all the way to the bank.

The stock transaction tax goes back a long way. A version helped fund the Civil War. The famous British economist, John Maynard Keynes, extolled in 1936 a securities transaction tax as having the effect of "mitigating the predominance of speculation over enterprise."

Professor Robert Pollin notes that after the 1987 stock market crash, securities-trading taxes "or similar measures" were endorsed by then Senate Minority Leader Bob Dole and even the first President Bush. Pollin estimates a one-half of 1 percent tax would raise about $350 billion a year. Other estimates are higher as volume of trading keeps increasing. Economist Dean Baker believes such revenues could "significantly reduce the income tax on labor. Better to tax something you like the least—speculation that destabilizes the economy—instead of human labor that builds an economy."

Source: *The Progressive Populist*, March 1, 2009 (by Ralph Nader)

Comment: Congressmen Peter DeFazio (D-OR) and Peter Welch (D-VT) have introduced legislation to tax derivatives, which are bets on bets, and other mystifying gambles by casino capitalism. The Democratic leaders, however hungry for revenue, are not pressing this bill toward enactment. Nor are the Republicans. Wall Street pours a lot of money into both major parties' campaign treasuries.

* * *

Keynes on our positive future. In a famous 1930 essay, "The Economic Possibilities for Our Grandchildren," the grandchild-less (and child-less) Keynes sketched a distant, Star-Trek-like future where once "the economic problem was solved," people could focus on the things that mattered most."

Source: *New York Times*, November 1, 2009, book review by Justin Fox.

Comment: "The economic problem" in the modern technological economy in the United States has not come close to being solved. Mass poverty, unemployment, shattered or no pensions, record consumer debt and home foreclosures are some examples. Yet productivity per worker, inflation adjusted, is at least fifteen times what it was in 1930. Something very systemic is wrong that keeps the just desserts of such productivity away from the workers who produce so much of it.

* * *

Last summer, there was a bunch of racket from a building of the Confined Animal Feeding Operation, or CAFO, about a half mile from our house. It turns out the ammonia and hydrogen sulfide from Cargill's 5,600 hogs had rotted out the steel roof of the building, causing it to collapse.... This CAFO business has never had a good prognosis. In fact, no bank would have touched the million-dollar loans to build them [the animals' housing] if the loans hadn't come with a guarantee of payment by the U.S. government.

The industry became more and more concentrated as the huge number of animals in confinement made it impossible for real farmers to compete. It also means pollution of the very worst kind. Each generation and type of CAFO has its own manure-handling system. These by-products can become certified as organic inputs for organic fields, and most of the organic products in the big box stores have been fertilized by effluent from CAFOs.

The genius of the business is that all the liability for the animals and buildings was laid on the operator of the CAFO [to whom livestock raising is subcontracted] while all the profits went to the (agribusiness) corporation. When times got tough, the corporation has simply cancelled contracts, and now the operators are stuck with empty buildings and plenty of debt.

For taxpayers, bankrupt CAFOs mean big cleanup headaches as the property goes to auction. Who's going to buy a pit full of manure? No one, of course. That means the country has to deal with the mess before it overflows into public waters or aquifers.

In Arkansas, Florida and North Carolina, more than 300 operators lost their contracts when Pilgrim's Pride declared Chapter 11 bankruptcy on December 1, 2008.

The best way to raise food is on family farms and the best way to rebuild failing counties is to train young farmers in sustainable techniques.

Source: *Progressive Populist*, March 15, 2009 (by Margot Ford McMillen)

Comment: The contracts that the agribusiness companies like Tyson Foods and Perdue make farmers sign to grow their chicks are so feudalistic that the relationship between the giants and the small feeders has been called "poultry peonage." If only more consumers knew how the beef and poultry they buy in their supermarket is raised....

* * *

Women still make 77 cents to the dollar a man makes for full time year around work... Employers are under no obligation to report pay statistics, and in most companies you can get fired for talking pay with co-workers.

[This provides the context for the following:] Governor Bill Richardson... has signed an executive order in New Mexico that is groundbreaking. Not only will the state as an employer have to study and report its own pay practices when it comes to gender and race, so will private sector companies that want state contracts.

Source: *The Progressive Populist*, March 15, 2009 (by Martha Burk)

In today's mad world, underpaid workers are bailing out banks and corporations run by overpaid, undertaxed bosses who milked their companies and our country like cash cows.

While workers across America were losing jobs, homes and health insurance, Merrill Lynch paid nearly 700 employees more than $1 million each in bonuses last year, amounting to a $3.6 billion bonus bonanza while Merrill lost $27 billion.

Workers have been sacrificing for years. Average worker paychecks are worth less now than in 1973, but CEOs and other rich Americans not only make much more, they pay less in taxes.

Average full-time workers made $41,198 in 1973 and $37,606 in 2008, adjusted for inflation.

CEOs made 45 times as much as workers in 1973 and more than 300 times as much as workers now.

Source: *The Progressive Populist*, March 15, 2009 (by Holly Sklar)

On January 30, Senator Claire McCaskill (D-Mo) said what a lot of us are thinking about Wall Street fat cats and how they are taking federal bailout money while handing out bonuses and pay raises to themselves.

"They don't get it," she said. "These people are idiots. You can't use taxpayer money to pay out $18 billion in bonuses ... What planet are these people on?"

McCaskill said those words on the Senate floor as she proposed legislation to cap executive pay at any company getting federal bailout money at $400,000, or the U.S. president's salary.

"Right now, they're on the hook to us," said McCaskill. "And they owe us something more than a fancy waste basket and a 15 million dollar jet. They owe us some common sense."

Source: *The Progressive Populist*, March 15, 2009 (by Randolph T. Holhut)

Comment: Senator McCaskill's bill died aborning. Shelved into oblivion by the Senate bulls. Into their waste basket. Netflix CEO Reed Hastings believes we should add a top tax rate of 50 percent on income above $1 million. Well, he won't be asked to testify anytime soon. Nor will Warren Buffett (net worth $50 billion) who in 2009 met with Democratic senators to urge them to raise taxes on the wealthy like him. He noted that he pays a lower tax rate than his secretary. The Democratic senators were either amused by this visiting Martian or backed away as if Buffett had drug-resistant tuberculosis.

* * *

Spinach, lettuce, jalapeno and serrano peppers. Common agricultural products have been severely tainted in recent years, leading to concerns about food-borne illness. And rightfully so. These outbreaks caused multiple death and more than a thousand illnesses nationwide. The Centers for Disease Control and Prevention (CDC) now estimates 76 million annual cases of food-borne illness, resulting in over 350,000 hospitalizations and 5,000 deaths.

With massive product recalls seemingly constant, coupled with rising public worry over Chinese and other foreign food imports, one would think that the federal government would have prioritized fixing its food system.

Our food safety regulations obviously are in need of a severe upgrade. ... The current division of food regulatory responsibility between the U.S. Department of Agriculture (USDA) and the Food and Drug Administration (FDA) is scientifically and organizationally irrational and indefensible. ... Food concerns have always been an afterthought at the FDA, which is primarily focused on drug regulations. ...The USDA, meanwhile, is fundamentally an agriculture promotion agency. Fixing the federal food safety system would alleviate this growing public concern.

Source: *The Progressive Populist*, March 15, 2009 (by Jonathan Cantu)

Comment: For many years, presidents have bewailed the weak food safety laws and small enforcement budgets, especially after fatal outbreaks of food poisoning. Bills languished in Congress, however, with neither the lawmakers nor the White House pressing for enactment. Finally, the House of Representatives has passed a so-so food safety bill and, not surprisingly, it quietly languished in the Senate graveyard waiting for more thousands of preventable American deaths before the Senate finally approved the legislation and President Obama signed it into law. Of course, with few exceptions, the lobbyists for giant food and food processing corporations are in no hurry.

* * *

Twenty-six crop scientists from land grant universities submitted a statement to the Environmental Protection Agency charging that biotechnology giants are preventing them from fully studying and reporting on the effectiveness and environmental impact of the industry's genetically altered seeds. On many crucial questions about the safety of these lab created crops, wrote the scientists, "No truly independent research can be legally conducted."

Why? Because the corporations and lobbyists and lawyers have rigged the rules so no studies can be done on their altered seeds without their permission, and even then no findings can be published without their okay. In short, those who profit from the spread of these unproven and dangerous seeds have a choke-hold on all research to evaluate their impact on our health and environment. The profiteers even have the potential, as one of the rebellious scientists put it, "to launder the data" that EPA relies on to authorize the use of the seeds.

Since these same corporations are now the major funders of university research on biotech crops, it is no small thing for scientists to speak out. As one bluntly says, "People are afraid of being blacklisted."

For information contact: www.organicconsumers.org

Source: *The Progressive Populist*, April 1, 2009 (by Jim Hightower)

Comment: Changing the nature of nature by commercial corporations requires rigorous examination by academic science to monitor the secretive commercial biases of corporate science. The EPA argues it does not have the legal authority to broaden academic research options for scientists. After the statement by the research scientists was issued, the American Seed Trade Association (ASTA) met with scientists to discuss "Academic Research Licenses (ARLs)." ARLs, however, do not provide an adequate remedy. Companies should not be the gatekeepers of scientific inquiry. Bruce Stutz, writing for Yale's Environment 360, reported that research scientists believe these restrictions preclude public scientists "from meeting their obligations to the American crop producer and ultimately the consumer." The system, as it now stands, "sets up an uneven relationship where industry partners may unduly influence the way research is designed and disseminated." Even once an agreement has been successfully negotiated, [the scientists] wrote, there's no guarantee the company won't withdraw its participation if the results appear to be unfavorable to its product." Source: e360.yale.edu/ May 13, 2010. For more information, see genewatch.org and ucsusa.org.

* * *

Media Blackout on Single-Payer Healthcare. Major newspaper broadcast and cable stories mentioning healthcare reform in the week leading up to President Obama's March 5 healthcare summit rarely mentioned the idea of a single-payer national health insurance program, according to a new study by Fairness and Accuracy in Reporting (FAIR.org). And advocates of such a system, two of whom participated in the White House summit, were almost entirely shut out, FAIR found.

Single-payer—a model in which healthcare delivery would remain largely private, but would be paid for by a single federal health insurance fund (much like Medicare provides for seniors and comparable to Canada's current system)—polls well with the public, who preferred it "two-to-one over a privatized system in a recent survey (*New York Times*/ CBS)."

Hundreds of stories in major newspapers and on NBC News, ABC News, CBS News, Fox News, CNN, MSNBC, NPR and PBS's *NewsHour* mentioned healthcare reform, according to a search of the Nexis database. Yet all but 18 of these stories made no mention of "single-payer" (or synonyms commonly used by its proponents such as "Medicare for all" or the proposed single-payer bill, HR676), and only five included the views of advocates of single-payer, none of which appeared on television. HR676 sponsored by Representative John Conyers (D-Mich) has more than 60 cosponsors and support from most AFL-CIO unions!

Source: *The Progressive Populist*, April 1, 2009

Congress must eliminate the private insurance industry and implement a national single-payer system if it wants to achieve true health care reform, two leading patient advocates told a U.S. House of Representatives subcommittee last week.

"Replacing private insurance companies with a national health insurance program could save $400 billion a year in excessive administrative costs, provide coverage to the 45 million people in the United States who are uninsured, and help prevent the more than 18,000 deaths a year from a lack of health insurance," said Dr. Sidney Wolfe, M.D. Public Citizen's acting president, and Dr. Steffie Woolhandler, M.D., professor at Harvard Medical School and co-founder of the Physicians for a National Heath Program.

"The real question is why should we tolerate the fragmented, highly profitable, administratively wasteful private health insurance industry any longer?" Wolfe told the Energy and Commerce Committee's Health Subcommittee.

"The health insurance and pharmaceutical industries thrive in the current decentralized system because there are no price controls, and insurance can turn away patients who are 'unprofitable,'" Wolfe said. "The insurance industry makes huge profits by denying care, paying out as little as it can and insuring only the healthiest patients," he said.

"Families with supposedly good coverage are just one serious illness away from financial ruin," Woolhandler told lawmakers. She cited a study she recently completed that showed that medical bills and illness contributed to 62 percent of all personal bankruptcies in 2007.

Source: *Corporate Crime Reporter*, June 29, 2009

Comment: A new peer-reviewed study in the *Journal of Public Health* (December 2009) raised the estimate of lives lost due to lack of health insurance in the U.S. to about 45,000 human beings a year. Dr. Woolhandler and Wolfe have extensive documentation for their conclusions.

* * *

"You know what really gets my goat about AIG shelling out 165 million of our tax dollars to the top executives of the very same division that destroyed the corporation? EVERYTHING, that's what! The arrogance, the greed, the secrecy, the inconceivable nincompoopery! Skunk farms don't stink as bad as this scandal. But one particular aspect of it hasn't received enough attention, and it really rubs me raw. It's the rationalization that was made by AIG's CEO and then docilely accepted as truth by Obama's top economic team. Their claim is that since the bonuses were part of the employment contracts of the executives, everyone must now bow down and meekly pay up.

"It would be legally difficult to prevent these contractually mandated payments," whimpered Treasury Secretary Tim Geithner.

"Come on, there are amoebas with more backbone than that! There is nothing sacred about a corporate contract—just ask union members and other workers. CEOs routinely abrogate legal contracts on wages, health care, and pensions for working folks. In fact, just last December, Washington demanded that car companies simply tear up their contracts with the United Auto Workers. Yet, suddenly we're to believe that AIG's contracts with these rich, incompetent investment bankers are so sacrosanct that even the President must stand impotently aside while they rob our public treasury?

"This is a defining moment on whether the Obamacans have the stuff to stand up to corporate power. They should confiscate these ill-gotten bonuses, then let the recipients sue to get the money back—if they dare."

Source: *The Progressive Populist*, April 15, 2009 (by Jim Hightower)

Comment: Taxpayer bailouts by definition abrogate all kinds of corporate contracts.

* * *

"The rich truly are different from you and me, for they are treated differently. I'm not talking about the merely affluent, but about the ultra-rich, those Wall Street elites who annually pocket tens of millions of dollars each through such financial entities as hedge funds and private equity firms. While you and I earn the bulk of our money from wages, the richy-rich don't receive anything as pedestrian as income. No, no, they have "gains."

Aside from the snoot factor, what's the difference? The tax code. Our ordinary income is taxed by the feds at a rate of up to 35 percent. The very rich, however, who haul in most of their income from capital gains, pay only 15 percent on this income.

They have lobbyists and are able to make impressive levels of campaign contributions to key politicians so the tax code has been deliberately perverted to benefit them.

Income is income, and the superrich deserve no special break just because they make their money from money. As Warren Buffett has asked, why should billionaire investors like him pay a lower tax rate "than our receptionists do or our cleaning ladies?" It's a question of fundamental fairness.

Source: *The Progressive Populist*, April 15, 2009 (by Jim Hightower)

For the first time since 1999, when the news broke that hundreds of people had died from asbestos-contaminated vermiculite mined in Libby, Montana, relatives and other victims were finally given the chance to confront those [W.R. Grace and Co.] former executives face to face [in a Missoula, Montana courtroom].

There are now more than 274 names on the Libby "death list," and another 1,200—out of a community of about 12,000—who have been diagnosed with asbestos-related diseases through a federal screening program. More cases are discovered every month.

Grace kept meticulous records, documenting the extreme potency of its particular asbestos fibers, the ease with which they became airborne, and the decline of the miners' health. It did this for three decades.

The federal government charges that the company and its executives conspired to violate the Clean Air Act by knowingly releasing asbestos into the air, endangering anyone who came in contact with it.

Lee Skramstad, who helped bring Libby's tragedy to the public's attention, long grieved over his unwitting role in exposing Little League ballplayers to asbestos as they played next to the vermiculite export plant where he worked. Les is gone now, a victim of mesothelioma, a rare, asbestos-related cancer.

Source: *The Progressive Populist*, April 15, 2009 (by Andra Peacock)

Comment: Libby, Montana, is one of numerous, devastated "company towns" around our country whose environment and workplace were poisoned by politically powerful, economically dominant corporations from the mining, chemical, textile, paper and energy industries.

* * *

Questions Our Health Care Debate Ignores. Amid all the reassuring blather, certain fundamental questions were not asked, as usual, because merely posting them might discomfort those same special interests and political leaders. Why do we spend so much more on healthcare, per capita, than other developed countries? Why do we achieve worse outcomes on several important measures than countries that spend far less? Why do we spend up to twice as much per person as countries that provide universal coverage while leaving as many as 50 million Americans without insurance?

The salience of those questions has grown over the past several decades, ever since President Truman first sought to create a universal health benefit program that resembled systems in Europe. Last month, the Organization for Economic Cooperation and Development (OECD) issued the latest in a long series of reports on our wasteful and cruel practices that ought to awaken a sense of national embarrassment....

As the study suggests, our grossly inflated and poorly managed health budget results from a variety of pathologies, including a greater prevalence of obesity and other chronic illness, a powerful pharmaceutical lobby that keeps prices high, and the profit-making imperative of the private insurance companies that still dominate American health policy more than four decades after we established coverage for the elderly.

Source: *The Progressive Populist*, April 15, 2009

Senator Bernie Sanders (I-VT) has proposed a law that would cap consumer loan rates at 15 percent. He noted that banks are getting money from the Federal Reserve at near zero percent interest rates but they turn around and charge Americans 20 percent to 30 percent and as high as 41 percent—more than double what they paid in interest in 1990.

"Recently, some major institutions such as Bank of America have informed responsible cardholders that their interest rates would be doubled to as high as 28 percent without explaining why the increase was taking place," he wrote. "The Bible has a term for this practice. It's called usury. And in *The Divine Comedy*, Dante Alighieri's epic poem, there was a special place reserved in the Seventh Circle of Hell for sinners who charged people usurious interest rates. Today, we don't need the hellfire and pitchforks, we don't need the rivers of boiling blood, but we do need a national usury law."

In 1991, a proposal to cap credit card interest rates at 14 percent passed the Senate by a vote of 74-19, but it never became law. Sanders noted that over the last decade, the financial sector has invested more than $5 billion in political influence purchasing in Washington. That sum covers some 3,000 lobbyists and huge amounts in campaign contributions. "The American people are thoroughly disgusted with the behavior of Wall Street, and they want their elected officials to respond to the greed of major financial institutions," Sanders wrote. "A cap on interest rates would be a good start. Do we have the courage?"

Source: *The Progressive Populist*, April 15, 2009

Comment: Sanders's bill in a heavily controlled Democratic Senate has gone nowhere. No Bernie, they don't have the courage.

Apparently, springtime is surge time in Afghanistan. President Obama is launching a new, expanded American adventure to "stabilize" this historically unstable, impoverished, warlord-state that's ruled by hundreds of fractious, heavily-armed tribal leaders. Some 36,000 American soldiers are already there, but it has not gone well for them. They've lost ground in a grinding, deadly war that's now in its eighth year, costing taxpayers $2 billion a week.

What to do? Spend more, cry the war hawks! So, Obama has announced a double-surge strategy for Afghanistan. First will be a surge of 17,000 more soldiers. Second will be a "civilian surge" of hundreds of U.S. economic development specialists, who will try to win the hearts and the cooperation of Afghan villagers through various efforts to lift their living standards.

But, look what's that coming over the hill? Why it's a third surge that Obama didn't mention: private military contractors! It was such profit-seeking outfits as Halliburton and Blackwater that ran rampant in Iraq, doing deep damage, yet here we go again with a private army in Afghanistan.

More than 71,000 of these corporate freelancers are already operating there, and hoards more are preparing to go as Pentagon spending ramps up for Obama's war. Pentagon Chief Robert Gates claims that these armed employees, i.e., mercenaries, are necessary to provide security for U.S. bases and convoys.

Say what? America has to hire private security firms to guard our Army? Yes, we're told, with no exception or even a wink at the absurdity of it.

Source: *The Progressive Populist*, May 1, 2009 (by Jim Hightower)

Comment: The surge of new U.S. soldiers has gone to 35,000 with even more corporate contractors who exceed the number of U.S. soldiers.

* * *

Let's Find Corporate America's Hidden Billions. It's time to reform offshore banking, and see what untaxed wealth big business is hiding in overseas tax shelters. The big claw-back will reach into quaint islands and mountainous principalities because the same banks, hedge funds and private equity firms responsible for the world financial meltdown keep their profits in those "secrecy places."... According to the Government Accountability Office of the U.S. Congress, nearly all of America's top 100 corporations maintain subsidiaries in countries identified as tax havens.

But what reason other than evasion could there be for Goldman Sachs Group to set up three subsidiaries in Bermuda, five in Mauritius, and 15 in the Cayman Islands? Why did Wachovia need 18 subsidiaries in Bermuda, three in the British Virgin Islands, and 16 in the Caymans? Why did Lehman Brothers need 31 subsidiaries in the Caymans? What do Bank of America's 59 subsidiaries in the Caymans actually do? Why does Citigroup need 427 separate subsidiaries in tax havens, including 12 in the Channel Islands, 21 in [the Isle of] Jersey, 91 in Luxembourg, 19 in Bermuda and 90 in the Caymans? What exactly is going on at Morgan Stanley's 19 subs in [the Isle of] Jersey, 29 subs in Luxembourg, 14 subs in the Marshall Islands, and its amazing 158 subs in the Caymans? (Don't expect to find out from Fox News Channel or the *New York Post*, because [owner] News Corporation has its own constellation of strange subsidiaries, including 33 in the Caymans alone). ...

None of these tax havens could exist without the connivance or at least the cooperation of the world's most powerful governments, which remain dominated by financial industry lobbyists even now.

Source: *The Progressive Populist*, May 1, 2009 (by Joe Conason)

Comment: Tax havens by the tax escapee corporations either increase taxes on working folks, reduce public services or increase government deficits. The return of hundreds of billions of dollars on the estimated $12 trillion in untaxed assets hidden around the world is a fundamental issue of fairness. For these corporations are still receiving the benefits of public services and protections but refusing to pay their fair share.

* * *

"Senate investigators estimate that Americans who hide assets in offshore bank accounts are failing to pay about $100 billion a year in taxes. In good times, that's grossly unfair and bad for the country. In times like these, it should be intolerable. ...

"UBS of Switzerland has acknowledged that as of September 30 it held about 47,000 secret accounts for Americans."

The *Times* piece goes on to note that UBS, while claiming to be very law-abiding and not willing to disclose the names of its American customers since, in so doing, they would be violating Swiss law, in February was found to be not so careful about American legality. They agreed to pay "$780 million in fines and restitutions" for illegally aiding Americans in concealing their assets.

The Tax Justice Network, a research and advocacy organization, had noted that UBS's wrongdoing is only the tip of the iceberg. It estimates $11.5 trillion of taxable assets are residing in such offshore havens.

Source: *New York Times*, editorial, March 14, 2009

Comment: The havens remain little disturbed, despite the empty furor by the large western nations in Europe and North America.

* * *

"Populist anger in America is the anger of dispossession," writes *Newsweek*'s Rick Perlstein. "The delinking of effort and reward has become all too manifest. That always makes Americans angry. We do not like to reward those who do not produce."

This is about abused customers. After decades of insults, they can't believe they're being made to save companies that treat them like crap.

I'm a calm person. Yet my most recent bank statement

featured three items that brought my blood to a fast boil. One was a $10 "income wire transfer fee." A newspaper that publishes this column paid for it by wiring the money to my account. The bank charged me ten bucks—for depositing money! Money that, by the way, they invest in what the banking industry calls "the overnight call float."

The same statement included a $3 fee for using an ATM that belongs to a different bank. Compared to my bank, loan sharks are sweethearts. If I take out $20 every day and pay $3 each time, that's 15 percent interest a day, or 5,475 percent a year. Did I mention that the fee was a mistake? I never use ATMs at other banks. To straighten out this $3, I'll have to waste my time explaining myself to someone at a call center in India, typing my account number into a keypad so I can repeat it by voice after waiting on hold.

I won't even mention the time they hit me with a $120 fine in a single month—12 separate fees at $10 a pop—for being stupid enough to use the line of credit they once begged me to take. I hate my bank. My bank is Citibank. Citibank sucks.

If Citibank wasn't an evil, customer-hating band of fee vultures, I might not be quite so annoyed at the fact that its parent company Citigroup had just received $20 billion in direct investment plus $306 billion in loan guarantees from the U.S. government (i.e., us). That's $1,100 per American citizen. ...

Source: *The Progressive Populist*, May 1, 2009 (by Ted Rall)

Comment: For more outrageous regular rip-offs, see *Gotcha Capitalism* by MSNBC's Brian Sullivan.

* * *

Twenty years ago, the Exxon Valdez supertanker spilled at least 11 million gallons of oil onto Alaska's pristine Prince William Sound. The consequences of the spill were epic and continue to this day, impacting the environment and the economy. ... Riki Ott, a marine toxicologist and commercial salmon "fisher'mam" from Cordova, Alaska, opens her book on the disaster, *Not One Drop*, with the words of Albert Einstein: "No problem can be solved from the same consciousness that created it."

The massive spill stretched 1,200 miles from the accident site, and covered 3,200 miles of shoreline and an incredible 10,000 square miles overall." By 1993, the fisheries had collapsed. Families lost their livelihoods after taking huge loans to buy boats and expensive fishing permits.

Complex litigation has dragged on for two decades and ExxonMobil is winning. There are 22,000 plaintiffs suing ExxonMobil. A jury awarded the plaintiffs $5 billion in damages, equal to what was, at the time, a year's worth of Exxon profits. This was cut in half by a U.S. appeals court, then finally lowered to just over $500 million by the U.S. Supreme Court. During the 20 years of court battles, 6,000 of the original plaintiffs have died.

Source: *The Progressive Populist*, May 1, 2009 (by Amy Goodman)

Comment: While the litigation was dragging on and the plaintiffs—commercial fishermen—were dragged down, two items are noteworthy. When the spill, enabled by a drinking skipper, occurred, gasoline prices in California shot up, thereby increasing Exxon's sales due to a perceived shortage. Also, ExxonMobil made $48 billion last year in profits.

* * *

What do you call it when arrogance, avarice and absurdity combine? Well, one name for it would be "Sallie Mae."

Despite the sweet name, Sallie is not a person. It's a giant financial corporation that is America's largest provider of student loans. It began in the 1970s as a government entity, but in 1997 it was privatized. Along with such other private lenders as Wells Fargo and Discover, Sallie Mae has used the "Family Education Loan" program to milk windfall profits from college students. The program is a corporate boondoggle, because the only thing it privatizes are the profits the lenders pocket through hefty fees they levy on students. The industry's losses, on the other hand, are socialized, for the government covers 97 percent of any loans that students fail to pay.

Because this absurd subsidy of private lenders rips off taxpayers while overcharging students, Obama has proposed ending it in favor of expanding the government's far-more-efficient and less costly program that loans directly to students. Cutting out the middleman would save taxpayers more than $9 billion a year, and redirect the saving to help students.

Going through private lenders is all the more absurd today because a government bailout is all that is keeping them afloat.

Source: *The Progressive Populist*, May 15, 2009 (by Jim Hightower)

Comment: In March 2010, President Obama signed a law that ended this taxpayer subsidy of the gouging student loan companies, like Sallie Mae, and afforded fuller opportunities for students to borrow money for their education from the Department of Education. Maybe now, Sallie Mae's big spending, massively overpaid CEO—Albert Lord—will have to rely more on himself and his company instead of milking Uncle Sam. Bad enough that Sallie Mae obtained the major contract to service these loans from the same Obama Administration. Bad corporate actors often seem to get their consolation prizes.

* * *

Chrysler Bailout a Stimulus... For Mexico? The Chrysler Corporation's survival has been assisted by federal efforts to provide it with billions in bridge loans and help it conclude a merger with Fiat. But Chrysler's expression of gratitude to its workers and the taxpayers of America: moving 850 jobs from its [award-winning] engine plant in Kenosha, Wisconsin to Mexico, where Chrysler has long had a major presence. Apparently the survival of the corporation does not mean the survival of the workers in Kenosha.

In Mexico, Chrysler will have the opportunity to exploit a workforce denied the right to organize independent unions. Thus, family-supporting jobs from Kenosha will be transformed into jobs that typically pay $1 or $2 an hour.

Meanwhile, southeastern Wisconsin will be dealt another devastating blow in its efforts to recover. More workers will lose buying power, and Obama's efforts to stimulate the economy will be, in effect, sabotaged.

Source: *The Progressive Populist*, June 1, 2009 (by Roger Bybee)

Comment: Taxpayers bail out Chrysler, which closes down more workers' jobs to go to Mexico, which depresses the community, which requires more taxpayer assistance and stimulus money. Taxpayers pay twice!

* * *

Corporate Crime Reporter: "Let's get an overview of U.S. apparel. Are the vast majority of U.S. shoes and clothes being made overseas?"

Ballinger: "Yes, the numbers are breathtaking. Only something like seven percent are made in the U.S.A."

Source: Interview of Jeffrey Ballinger, Ph.D., a pioneer in the global anti-sweatship movement, by the *Corporate Crime Reporter*, November 16, 2009

Goldman Sachs (which has us taxpayers on the hook for more than $50 billion in its bailout package) breathlessly announced a dazzling profit of $1.8 billion for the first quarter. The dazzle dimmed, however, when it was learned that Goldman had altered its definition of "quarter," shifting its normal December-to-March quarter ahead one month, thus disappearing December. That was a month in which the bank lost $1.5 billion, so scrubbing it gave the revised calendar a neat banker buff job.

Source: *The Progressive Populist*, June 1, 2009 (by Jim Hightower)

Outside medicine, conflicts of interest are not uncommon.

Legislators vote the lobbyist-way. Mortgage brokers profit at the signing of the contract, regardless of the solvency of the borrower. Investment firms' researchers tout securities that the firms are selling. The consumer, generally unaware, suffers.

Patients are just as vulnerable. Has a physician recommended drug x because of a persuasive article in a medical journal? If so, did an industry ghost-writer author the article, under the byline of a credentialed specialist? Did industry spokespeople influence the guidelines that suggest what drugs to use, and when? Did the blitz of information on a new medical device drown out the negative reports? Did the vendor that sponsored the continuing education seminar skew the presentation? With a drawer of samples, is a physician less likely to prescribe a generic drug? Or no drug?

The Institute of Medicine recently reviewed the infiltration of vendors into medical decision-making. The report recommended some actions on the part of physicians, hospitals and health providers: stop accepting the flood of freebies, from pens to pads to cruises. It recommended that the medical journals ask authors to disclose their ties to the industry. Most crucially, it recommended that Congress institute a national reporting system, where the three mega-vendor-companies that market pharmaceuticals, medical devices, and biotechnology treatments disclose their funding to the public. We, the patients, should be able to see what company gave what amount to patient advocacy groups, to physicians, to research institutions, to hospitals. Justice Louis Brandeis praised the disinfecting nature of "sunlight" in the public arena.

Source: *The Progressive Populist*, June 15, 2009 (by Joan Retsinas)

Katie Hebert, age four, is a very sick girl. She gets seizure-like attacks that can last 11 hours from an undiagnosed neuro-developmental disorder. She is deaf in one ear, has a feeding disorder and requires daily medication for asthma. In her short life, she has been rushed to the emergency room six times and hospitalized twice. She was put at even greater risk when she lost her health coverage, meaning no more regular doctor visits, weekly therapy or attention from specialists.

Katie's father tried, but couldn't afford the roughly $1,000 a month, about 30 percent of his salary, to pay for the plan from his employer. And even if he could have afforded the insurance, it would not have covered all of Katie's needs. Other private insurers would not accept Katie because of her pre-existing conditions.

The only alternative was the Texas Children's Health Insurance Program (CHIP). But her father made $260 a month above the limit that would enable Katie and her older brother, Nathan, seven, to qualify for CHIP. Mr. Hebert is a reliable worker who has helped maintain the computers for a banking system in Pasadena, Texas, over the past six years. He requested a voluntary pay cut in an already modest income so his children could get insurance, but his employer didn't respond. The family eventually spent down its income by paying for unnecessary childcare to become financially eligible for CHIP.

That wasn't the end of it, however. When Katie's dad got an automatic three percent cost of living raise, the family's income once again exceeded the CHIP limit, this time by $20.54 a month. While her father went through the process of having his wages lowered, Katie was without health coverage—again.

Katie is one of millions of children in working families who face impossible barriers to obtaining health coverage imposed by insurance companies that make enormous profits and pay their CEOs and top managers fat compensation packages. They decide who gets coverage, what medical treatment they'll pay for, and how much they pay doctors and hospitals. The premiums these companies charge and these restrictions are major reasons why 46 million Americans are without health insurance-including nine million children.

Source: *The Progressive Populist*, June 15, 2009 (by Marian Wright Edelman)

Comment: People living in many Western countries starting with Canada, would read the above with utter disbelief or utter revulsion. Such commercial cruelty and cowardly governments give new meaning to the saying "Only in America." Year after year. Obamacare is now law but coverage won't take effect until 2014, leaving over 24 million people still without coverage. Four years is more than enough time to give Aetna's, Cigna's, and United HealthCare's attorneys time to learn how to game and circumvent restrictions on their greed. Four years will also claim 180,000 lives lost due to absence of health insurance for treatment, plus mean countless illnesses and injuries untreated. Four more years should be used to speed full Medicare for all—everybody in, nobody out—through Congress. No people in all these Western countries die because they cannot afford health insurance—for they are all insured from the day they are born!

* * *

The Pentagon continues to pay Halliburton and its former giant subsidiary, KBR, huge contract sums despite repeated corporate overbilling, faulty products and services, and bribery. This continues in spite of documentation by Pentagon investigators and auditors of gigantic overcharges and waste, spiraling claims of workplace negligence, including faulty electrical wiring that led to deaths and injuries on bases [in Iraq] KBR built and a failure to provide adequately clean water supplies to the troops. ... According to Senator Byron Dorgan, documents show that KBR was paid huge bonuses by the Pentagon for this work, much of it after the allegation became public.

Source: *The Progressive Populist*, July 1-15, 2009 (by Pratap Chatterjee)

Comment: For a fuller rendition of these companies' predations see Mr. Chatterjee's book, *Halliburton's Army: How a Well-Connected Texas Oil Company Revolutionized the Way America Makes War*. Until 2000, vice-president Dick Cheney was the CEO of Halliburton and continued to receive pension payments.

* * *

"Stop Mountain Top Removal." Obama speaketh, and it was good.

"We have to find more environmentally sound ways of mining coal than simply blowing the tops off mountains," he proclaimed. And yes, in the mountains and down through all the valleys of the ancient land of Appalachia, hearts were filled with joy, for here was a prophet of hope who was signaling that a change was coming—at last, the endtime was at hand for the brutish coal-mining method called "mountaintop removal."

With the top third of these awesome, forested mountains reduced to rubble, the coal barons use giant machines to strip out seams of coal, and then they simply shovel the rubble and toxic coal waste down the mountainsides, burying the valleys and streams below. It was a desecration, but the love of mammon made it the law of the land.

On May 15, it was announced that Barack Obama's Environmental Protection Agency had quietly approved 42 of 48 new Appalachian mining permits sought by the coal barons. Say what?...

Once he was in office, coal executives, lobbyists and other enthusiasts for bank-and-shovel mining went to work on him.

The industry rationalizes its greed in the name of creating jobs for this hard-hit region, but mountaintop removal relies on dynamite and huge machines, not workers. In fact, thousands of mining jobs have been lost as corporations switched to this method. In all of Appalachia, there are only 19,000 jobs connected to every form of surface mining, and the tiniest fraction of those are in mountaintop removal. A much brighter job future is to develop Appalachia's boundless green-energy potential—a blue-green initiative that's supposed to be one of Obama's top priorities.

Source: *The Progressive Populist*, July 1-15, 2009 (by Jim Hightower)

"A college student who bid on and won more than $1.8 million in federal oil and gas leases last year without the intent or ability to pay will not be allowed to argue in court that he acted out of necessity to protect the environment, a federal judge ruled on Monday.

"The student, Tim DeChristopher, 27, an economics major at the University of Utah, faces up to five years in prison and huge fines," according to the *New York Times*, both for interfering with an auction and for making false claims.

DeChristopher felt compelled to engage in this deception because of the dire environmental effects of the drilling and the part the oil and gas industries play in global warming, the *Times* stated.

Source: *New York Times*, November 16, 2009 (by Kirk Johnson)

Comment: On March 3, 2011, Mr. DeChristopher was convicted of disrupting a federal auction and making false statements on federal forms to enter the auction. In July, he was sentenced to two years in prison and fined $10,000. Consider how the natural resource laws are skewed to the mining industry. The 1872 Mining Act allows domestic or foreign mining companies to go on our (federal) land, and if they discover any hard rock minerals (such as gold, silver, molybdenum), they can go the Department of the Interior in Washington, D.C., and gain ownership of those minerals for $5 per acre. Barrick Corporation from Canada over a decade ago was given ownership by the federal government of $9 billion of gold on our (federal land) in Nevada for less than $30,000 to purchase the acreage over it, with no royalties back to Uncle Sam. And the taxpayers often have to clean up the cyanide-laced wastes after the mine is exhausted. See the difference.

* * *

In June 2009, a 29-state outbreak of E. coli was traced to a Virginia food plant owned by Nestlé, the Swiss-based food giant. The particular perpetrator is Nestlé's very popular, refrigerated Toll House cookie dough. It's like being poisoned by someone you love.

The Food and Drug Administration is investigating the mystery of how E. coli got into chocolate chip cookie dough, and they don't yet have an answer. But the incident has uncovered a silent accomplice in E. coli's poisonous rampage: our food safety laws. Rules supposedly meant to protect consumers have been perverted to protect the big manufacturers. The FDA does send inspectors into these food plants, but—get this—the corporations can dictate what our inspectors can and cannot look at. It turns out that Nestlé has been less than cooperative, refusing to allow FDA inspectors to review consumer complaints and to inspect the company's program for preventing food contamination. It has also denied access to pest-control records and refused to let inspectors photograph any part of the plant.

Source: *The Progressive Populist*, August 1, 2009 (by Jim Hightower)

Comment: The new food safety law, signed on January 4, 2011, by President Obama, gives the FDA more authority in such situations. Whether the FDA will use that authority remains to be seen. The Department of Transportation has had powerful subpoena authority, but did not use it for years during the deadly Toyota sudden acceleration debacle.

* * *

The administration has rolled out its financial reform plan, which President Obama accurately calls "the boldest set of reforms in financial regulation in 75 years ..." The banking lobby has reacted like wasps whose hive has been hit by a stick, swarming out to fend off the threat. First target of their sting is the proposed Consumer Financial Protection Agency, designed to defend consumers from the serial abuses of credit card companies, payday lenders, mortgage brokers and the like. This assault on the consumer agency reveals how much the banking lobby has already won. Most notable about the administration's plan is what was left out. Nothing real is done about compensation schemes.

Exotic derivatives and credit default swaps are not banned.

Ratings agencies are still paid by the financial houses they are supposed to rate.

Banks too big to fail are to be monitored, not broken up.

Oversight of the system is entrusted to the Federal Reserve, which was designed to insulate money center banks from the democracy.

No mention is made of a tax on securities transactions that would both put a damper on excessive speculation and raise a ton of money to help repay some of the staggering costs of the crisis the speculators caused....

The banks, even on life support, have big-time clout in Washington. They blocked the effort to give bankruptcy judges the right to renegotiate mortgages of distressed families. They torpedoed legislation to put a lid on credit card interest rates. "It's hard to believe," Illinois Senator Richard Durbin said in frustration, but the banks are "still the most powerful lobby on Capitol Hill. And they frankly own the place."

Source: *The Progressive Populist*, August 1, 2009 (by Robert Borosage)

Secretary of Defense Robert Gates and President Obama have been accused of gutting America's defenses and even undercutting our troops in a time of war. [Accused by Sarah Palin, for example.] Would you be surprised to learn that the Obama defense budget is actually $20 billion bigger than the last one signed by President George W. Bush? Moreover, the actual cuts proposed to specific programs are minor in scale compared to the $700 billion-plus total. And when you consider a report from the nonpartisan Government Accountability Office showing $300 billion in taxpayer money wasted on over-budget weapon systems, the idea that we are somehow "cutting" defense seems exaggerated. The truth is that shoveling billions at the Pentagon is a big business with lobbyists, politicians and officials invested in making sure that the money continues to move with no questions asked. Even Secretary Gates' intention of reining in the dysfunctional weapons procurement process is being administered by a former lobbyist for Raytheon, a major defense contractor, who had previously fought against reform.

Source: *The Progressive Populist*, August 1, 2009 (by Vice

Admiral Jack Shanahan (rd.), former commander of the U.S. Second Fleet)

Washington's best and brightest, working 24/7 on health insurance reform, are whining. ... The team—call them Team A—is debating key policy decisions. Its members are private sector bigwigs from the industries that benefit from the status quo, abetted by the Congressional and Senate solons whose campaigns they have generously supported....

Why not send in Team B? I bet they could succeed.

For a start, recruit a few uninsured people for this team. Ask the people who clean the houses, cut the grass, and take care of the children of Team A honchos. Visit an unemployment office, drawing from those whose employers downsized or declared bankruptcy. Try employees who can't afford their companies' policies. Ask parents who have been dropped from their states' Children's Health Insurance rolls. Look closer to home, at the legions of "contract workers" that government and industry hire to avoid paying for insurance.

Next, recruit a few people who have private coverage, but are not singing its praises. Try one or two "medically bankrupt" people—the ones driven to bankruptcy not by predatory mortgages or pink slips, but by medical bills. ... Retrieve a few names from those people who are bureaucratically trapped, trying to get somebody to explain why treatment x or drug x was denied. ... Recruit some people with chronic illnesses who have exceeded their insurers' caps.... Invite a few foreigners onto this team, from those countries in the developed world that cover all their citizenry at a lower per capita cost than we do in the United States.

Source: *The Progressive Populist*, August 1, 2009 (by Joan Retsinas)

Have you received your thank-you note? I'm still waiting for mine. More than a year into the Wall Street bailout, I've yet to get any sort of "thank you" from even a single one of the big banks that you and I propped up with $12 trillion in direct giveaways, indirect giveaways, government guarantees and sweetheart loans. You'd think their mommas would've taught them better. ...

Far from showing appreciation, the largest banking chains are now going out of their way to stiff us. They are quietly slipping new gotchas into our monthly credit card bills and banks statements. In June, for example, Bank of America abruptly raised its fee for a basic checking account by 50 percent. Citibank jacked up the interest rate on some of its cards to 29.99 percent. And J.P. Morgan Chase more than doubled the required payment on its cards.

Across the board, fees have skyrocketed to their highest levels on record, including assessments for such common occurrences as overdrafts (as high as $39), stop-payment actions ($39—double what it was ten years ago), balance transfers (up more than 50 percent in the past year), and ATM use (nearly doubled in 10 years). ...

The truth is, they are socking it to their customers for two reasons: 1) they can, and 2) fee hikes are a shifty way to snatch enormous levels of new income for themselves without doing anything to earn it.

Source: *The Progressive Populist*, August 15, 2009 (by Jim Hightower)

Comment: Banks get away with this private taxation because there is no regulation of these super-fleecing fees or penalties, and second, because there is no freedom of contract. Almost all banks have the same fine print chaining you so you can't find a competitive contract. You just sign on the dotted line. Try changing any of the fine print before you open an account and see what the response is from the bank.

* * *

Mitch Daniels, governor of Indiana, was announcing his hallmark plan to outsource that state's administration of food stamps, Medicaid and other welfare benefits for poor folks. ... IBM was given a $1.1 billion contract from the state to take charge. Taxpayers, boasted the governor, will reap "a billion dollars in savings," while low-income families will enjoy the stellar service of the private sector.

More than two years into the task, IBM's stumbles and fumbles include lost paperwork, frustrating runarounds, poorly-trained staff, inadequate equipment, and the rejection of qualified applicants. The rate of mishandled food-stamp cases, for example, has more than tripled since IBM took over.

Update: To try to fix this mess, the state has now issued a list of 200 reforms that IBM must achieve, giving it until September to shape up. ... A state official says bluntly: "It's possible we'd have to cancel the contract."

Source: *The Progressive Populist*, August 15, 2009 (by Jim Hightower)

Banks Misused Bailout Funds. Many of the banks that got federal aid to support increased lending have instead used the money to make investments, repay debts or buy other banks, the inspector general of the bank bailout reported. Of 360 surveyed banks, 110 invested at least some of the money, 52 repaid debts and 15 used the funds to buy other banks. Roughly 80 percent, or 300 banks, said at least some of the money supported new lending.

Since October, the government has invested more than $200 billion in more than 600 banks under the Troubled Assets Relief Program (TARP). The program was supposed to increase the capital reserves of healthy banks, allowing them to make more loans, but from the beginning the government invested in troubled banks, such as Citigroup, that had publically announced intentions to reduce lending.

Source: "Dispatches," *The Progressive Populist*, August 15, 2009

Why Support Corporations That Don't Support Us?

Yes, our overall economy is a wreck—but you'll be glad to know that one business sector is booming: outsourcing American jobs to India. It almost makes you burst with patriotic pride, doesn't it? Even as unemployment nears 10 percent across our country, more and more U.S. corporations are literally cutting out on America's middle class, eliminating employees here as they shift their operations and jobs to low-wage workers 8,000 miles away.

Some in Washington talk about measures to keep good jobs in the USA, but greedheaded corporate executives lobby furiously to prevent any action. "Anything that stops the globalization activity," declares David Cote, CEO of Honeywell, "will be harmful." Oh? To whom? Perhaps to him, but not to Honeywell's American workers, who're suffering from Honeywell's pell mell pursuit of globalization. Cote has been closing plants here and eliminating hundreds of jobs at the same time he is investing $50 million to build a new R&D center in India that will hire 3,000 people.

Likewise, Hewlett-Packard is offing some 15,000 American employees, even as it is establishing "HP Software Universities" in eight Indian cities to train thousands of new high-tech workers there. Why not invest in training Americans? Because those running these multibillion-dollar outfits feel no allegiance to America, thus they feel free to abandon our middle class—for nothing more noble than lining their own pockets by paying low wages to workers abroad.

Insurance giants, drug makers, corporate law firms, media conglomerates, and others are joining in the abandonment. They say "it's less costly" for them. Never mind what it cost their country.

If these profiteers have no loyalty to us, why be loyal to them? We should yank away all subsidies and every single benefit they get from America.

Source: *The Populist Progressive*, September 1, 2009 (by Jim Hightower)

Comment: Certainly drop all tax breaks and foreign investment subsidies from Washington.

* * *

"Guided by Mr. Bush's dictum that 'government should be market-based,' federal operations under his administration were encouraged to outsource wherever they could," according to a *Wall Street Journal* report by Thomas Frank.

Frank shows that, under the Bush regime, federal agencies would get higher marks the more of their own duties they could hand off to private contractors. The result, as shown in statistics published in 2005 by Paul C. Light of New York University, is that there are four times as many contract, private-sector employees as there are actual government workers on the federal payroll.

And, as Frank tartly remarks, the performance of the private sector has not been as promised. This shift was sold to the public as a way to deliver quality, but, he says, "instead we witnessed the most spectacular government failure in years."

Witness, for example, the over-billing, and shoddy services American received from private contractors in Iraq or in connection to disaster relief provided to the region struck by Hurricane Katrina.

These and other scandals related to the private sector contractors who are plundering rather than providing service received harsh words from President Obama, who noted, "Far too often [government] spending is plagued by massive cost overruns, outright fraud, and the absence of oversight and accountability."

The president says this situation must be remedied, but results are not yet in. Frank ends optimistically, stating, "We can only hope he means [there will be] a thorough and public examination of the most outrageous contractor misconduct of the last eight years."

Source: *The Wall Street Journal*, March 11, 2009 (by Thomas Frank)

Comment: There are few public indications that anything has changed since President Obama's declared reform effort. This is so even though the media published numerous exposes of contractors gouging and overspending both here and abroad, especially in Iraq and Afghanistan, big, big time. For a jarring experience, watch the documentary *Iraq for Sale: The War Profiteers* (Brave New Films). See how your tax dollars are being hijacked beyond your wildest nightmares.

* * *

In the mid-nineties, tobacco-giant Phillip Morris and its

corporate allies secretly launched a nationwide campaign to rig the rules of judicial access in their favor. Philip Morris itself put up $16 million in 1995 to hire a PR firm to create faux "grassroots" fronts in every state under the banner of Citizens Against Lawsuit Abuse.

These CALA front groups (which continue to demonize consumer lawyers and fight for new laws to take away our fundamental right to seek legal redress against corporations that injure us) are funded and controlled through another corporate front named ATRA, the American Tort Reform Association. Its backers include a who's who of big business brand names, from Anheuser-Busch to Wyeth Pharmaceuticals.

The lawsuit abuse groups are innately dishonest, not only because they deliberately hide their special-interest parentage from the public, but also because they're not really against abusive lawsuits. It's only legal actions against big corporations that get their knickers in a knot. On the other hand, when those same corporations turn their powerhouse legal departments against the hoi polloi (consumers, small businesses, environmental groups, etc), we never hear a peep of complaint from a CALA about abuse.

Source: *The Progressive Populist*, November 15, 2009 (by Jim Hightower)

Comment: It is getting harder and harder for regular Americans to sue the Big Boys in either state courts or the federal courts. Business lobbies have gotten past many restrictions on the people's day in court and right of trial by jury by campaign- money-greased legislators tying the hands of the only people who see, hear and assess the cases: the judges and juries in the courtroom.

* * *

Look at this from Garrison Keillor. A person saves his money like he was brought up to do and he salts it away in a safe CD or Treasury note or municipal bond and it pays him a measly 2 percent interest. Why? Because Federal Reserve has decreed we gotta have low interest to save the high-fliers and speculators who almost brought the roof crashing down a year ago, and they pour money into Goldman Sachs, and these killer sharks walk away with a hundred billion in bonuses and meanwhile guys are losing their shirts in the dairy business. "What's the deal here?" [Said to Garrison Keillor by an "old guy in a plaid shirt"] ... "I'm serious," he says. "You drive out west of here and you see headlights in the fields at midnight, guys putting in 16 hour days combining beans; and back east you've got people in offices with a phone in each hand, moving money around, not creating a damn thing, just playing a game, and the government can't do enough for them. Where's the fairness in that?"

Source: *The Progressive Populist*, November 15, 2009 (by Garrison Keillor)

Comment: And people in Washington and Wall Street wonder why people in the hinterland are so angry!

* * *

Time Out For Fresh Air! Steelworkers Work with World's Largest Worker-Owned Co-op. The United Steelworkers and the Spanish-based Mondragon International S.A. have announced a framework agreement for collaborating to establish Mondragon cooperatives in the manufacturing sector within the U.S. and Canada.

The manufacturing cooperatives that will be created in the U.S. will adopt the collective bargaining principles of the Mondragon worker-ownership model of "one worker, one vote." The Agreement was reached on October 27.

The Spanish co-op was started in 1956 in the Basque rural town of Mondragon by a visionary priest. Today, it has some 100,000 cooperative members in 260 enterprises and has a presence in more than 40 countries.

The co-op has its own university, bank and social security system. In 2008, it reached annual sales of more than 16 billion euros ($23.5 billion). It is the seventh largest enterprise in Spain and the world's largest industrial workers cooperative.

"We see today's agreement as an historic first step toward making union co-ops a viable business model that can create good jobs, empower workers and support communities in the United States and Canada," said USW International President Leo Gerard. "Too often we have seen Wall Street hollow out communities by shedding jobs and closing plants."

The Steelworkers' bold and unprecedented deal with Mondragon is a remarkable achievement on at least two counts. It can open up a new foreign market for U.S. manufactured goods. It can provide good-paying jobs by creating a chain of co-op stores that are committed to union standards. It also can strengthen labor's role in the global marketplace.

The USW has opted to globalize its operations by forming alliances with its foreign counterparts, unions that represent employees at the same global companies where USW members work."

Source: *The Progressive Populist*, December 1, 2009 (by Harry Kelber)

"We Need a Tax on Speculators. In the midst of the worst recession since the Great Depression, Goldman Sachs is having a banner year.... Goldman churned out $3 billion in profits in the third quarter, while the economy shed 768,000 jobs, and home foreclosures set a record... Colin Barr, from [CNNMoney.com,] writes that Goldman's "eye-popping profit" resulted "as revenue from trading rose fourfold from a year ago." Really. Revenue from trading? Didn't we bail out Goldman and the other Wall Street banks so they could make loans, take deposits and keep our money safe?

That is what banks used to do, but today the big Wall Street Money comes from short-term speculation in currency transactions, commodities, stocks and derivatives for the banks' own accounts. And here's the beauty of it: the Wall Street speculators have managed to trade in practically the only products left on the planet that are not subject to a sales tax. While parents in California are now paying 9 percent sales tax on their children's school bags and shoes, Goldman is paying zero tax to sustain its gambling habit. Race track winnings and other forms of gambling are taxed at up to 25 percent. But stock market trades get off scot free.

That helps explain Goldman's equally eye-popping tax bracket. What would you guess; 50 percent? 30 percent? Not even close. In 2008, Goldman Sachs paid a paltry 1 percent in taxes—less than clerks at WalMart..."

Leaders from France, Germany, and the European Commission endorsed putting a speculation tax on the agenda at the G20 meeting in Pittsburgh in September... Derivatives are essentially bets on whether the value of currencies, commodities, stocks, government bonds or virtually any other product will go up or down. Derivative bets can cause shifts in overall market size reaching $40 trillion in a single day. Just how destabilizing short-term speculation can be—and just how lucrative a tax on it could be—is evident from the mind-boggling size of the market: $743 trillion globally in 2008. Another arresting fact is that just five super-rich commercial banks control 97 percent of the U.S. derivatives market: JPMorgan Chase & Co., Goldman Sachs Group Inc., Bank of America Corp., Citigroup Inc. and Wells Fargo & Co.

Source: *The Progressive Populist*, December 15, 2009 (by Ellen Brown)

Comment: One effect of the self-inflicted Wall St. collapse and federal bailout is to concentrate more assets and deposits in fewer and fewer giant banks, making them, in the eyes of Washington politicians, even more "too big to fail," and, apparently, "too big to tax." A speculation tax can raise hundreds of billions of dollars a year and reduce the tax burdens on working people. Are you interested enough to act?

* * *

"So Much for the Mother Country. The United States and Britain voiced disagreement Saturday over a proposal that would impose a new tax on financial transactions to support future bank rescues.

"Prime Minister Gordon Brown of Britain said such a tax on banks should be considered as a way to take the burden off taxpayers during periods of financial crisis." As the *Times* reports, Brown's statement came at a meeting of the Group of 20, a consortium of finance ministers from the EU and 19 other industrialized countries, who are attempting to get a handle on the current economic crisis.

While Brown was looking to a new direction in helping lessen the crisis, the United States Treasury secretary, Timothy F. Geithner, would have nothing to do with it, saying he was against any such new tax.

Source: *New York Times*, November 8, 2009 (by Julia Werdigier)

It happened as I watched a 50-something woman walk out, after spending several hours being attended to by volunteer doctors. "She's decided against treatment. A reasonable decision under the circumstances," the doctor tells us as she heads for the next patient. The president of the board of the National Association of Free Health Clinics tells me why: "It's stage four breast cancer, her body is filled with tumors." I don't know when that woman last saw a doctor. But I do know that if she had health insurance, the odds she would have seen a doctor long ago are much higher, and her chances for an earlier diagnosis and treatment would have been far greater.

After watching for hours as the patients moved through the clinic, it was hard to believe I was in America.

Eighty-three percent of the patients they see are employed, they are not accepting other government help on a large scale, are not "welfare queens" as some would like to have us believe. They are tax-paying, good, upstanding citizens who are trying to make it and give their kids a better life just like you and me.

Ninety percent of the patients who came through the November 14 clinic had two or more diagnoses.

Eighty-two percent had a life threatening condition such as cardiovascular diseases, diabetes, and hypertension. They are victims of a system built with corporate profits at its center, which long ago forgot the usual imperative that should drive us to show compassion to our fellow men and women....

What does it say about us as a nation of people who can live in a country so rich and yet allow this to continue?

Source: *The Progressive Populist*, January 1-15, 2010

"A study to be released Monday of financial news coverage this year found that government, Wall Street and a small handful of story lines got the bulk of the attention while much less was paid to the economic troubles of ordinary people.

"The study, by the Pew Research Center's Project for Excellence in Journalism, also found that when the stock market rebounded from its lows and pitched battles in Washington ended, the news media turned their attention away from economic coverage." This important piece from the *New York Times* gives further background on the Pew report, indicating it was grounded in the examination of 10,000 news reports from February 1 to August 31, looking at daily papers, Web sites, radio broadcasts and on those appearing on cable and network TV.

The breakdown of coverage showed nearly 40 percent of economic news looked at the woes of the banking and auto industries or the federal stimulus package. A much less generous 12 percent was devoted to the unemployment and the mortgage meltdown. As to news that focused on the effect of the crisis on average Joes and Janes, that amounted to a paltry "5 percent of the economic coverage."

Source: *New York Times*, October 5, 2009 (by Richard Perez-Pena)

"Large, well-capitalized companies have no problem finding credit. Small businesses, on the other hand, have never had a harder time getting a loan," writes Meredith Whitney in the *Wall Street Journal*.

Surveying the credit situation since the financial downturn, she notes that there has been a severe contraction of credit, evident in both the slashing of credit-card lines, from which small businesses draw much of their funding, by 25 percent since last year, and the diminution of small business loans. Overall, in the last couple of years, credit extended to consumers and small business has diminished by "trillions of dollars."

Whitney reminds readers that, though these small businesses are diminutive in size, they play a large part in American commerce, supplying 50 percent of the country's jobs and accounting for 38 percent of GDP. Moreover, time and again, major innovations have gotten their start in these smaller firms.

Still, while the government has opened its wallet to the businesses classified as "too big to fail," it leaves "unassisted and at significant disadvantage," the businesses, which, it seems, are too small to save, much to our nation's misfortune.

Source: *Wall Street Journal* October 3, 2009 (by Meredith Whitney)

Comment: The author points out that Apple, Dell, McDonald's, and Starbucks were all started as small businesses.

* * *

"These days, it seems, there is no shortage of recommendations for fixing the way bonuses are paid to executives at big public companies.

"Well, I have my own recommendations. Scrap the whole thing. Don't pay any bonuses. Nothing."

So begins a strongly worded piece in the *Wall Street Journal* by McGill management professor Henry Mintzberg. He goes on to argue that the current way executive bonuses are handed out is not only scandalous in terms of the size of the monies these top players get; but that, even if legal, they are ultimately corrupt and corrupting. Indeed, they are a feature of our current system that must take major responsibility for "undermining our large corporations and bringing down the global economy."

Mintzberg labels the reigning system a form of gambling, one which operates with a stacked deck in the sense that the executives gathering in the bonuses can't lose.

For one, "they play with other people's money," that of their companies' stockholders. Second, they reap their windfalls as soon as their firms experience short-term elevation of their stock prices, which means the executives cash in "not when they win so much as when it appears they are winning." Maneuvers these executives may have made to lift company stock prices may not be (and often aren't) ones that are best for their firms' long-term viability. Third, even if their bets fail and companies' values drop, resulting in the executives being fired. No problem. They still have "golden parachutes" provided for in their original contracts, which are large severance packages that amount to ensured bonuses even for failure.

And, fourthly, many executives get paid, as the author notes, simply for "drawing cards." This occurs, for instance, when they obtain a bonus "when they have signed a merger, before anyone can know if it will work out. Most mergers don't."

Lastly, the author explains, with the "retention bonus," executives are paid simply for staying at the company.

It would be far better, Mintzberg contends, if executives were paid just like anyone else, with a straight salary, not with lavish perks and bonuses. These emoluments are ultimately self defeating, Mintzberg concludes, in that "if you do pay bonuses, you get the worst person in that chair."

Source: *Wall Street Journal*, November 30, 2009 (by Professor of Management Henry Mintzberg, McGill University)

Comment: Executive bonuses are approved by rubber-stamp boards of directors chosen by—you guessed it—these very same executives.

* * *

"Perilous Fun. For parents wanting to provide their children some good, clean off-roading fun, the Fushin, a smaller-than-normal, all-terrain vehicle [A.T.V.], seemed just the thing. Except the Chinese import with jaunty yellow paint and a low $250 price tag was missing one feature: front brakes.

"In the $5 billion market for A.T.V.'s, the skyrocketing

growth of Chinese imports is becoming the latest challenge for the Consumer Product Safety Commission, which is starting a global campaign to improve the safety of a product that kills more people —about 900 a year—than any of the 15,000 other products the commission regulates."

The *Times* story goes on to report that Fushin's A.T.V.'s, along with posing a danger due to their lack of brakes, also have sharp handlebars, which could wound riders, and contain lead parts, which make them pollution hazards.

This is no small problem in that, according to the commission, about 100 children die and 40,000 are hospitalized each year in A.T.V. accidents.

While the Chinese company is recalling some of its vehicles, and U.S. Customs is forbidding the entrance of others deemed unsafe—a few weeks back Customs seized a shipload in Houston— many complain that the commission only clamps "down on problem products after the damage has been done and reported."

Sue Rabe, a mother whose 10-year-old was killed in an A.T.V. accident and who founded Concerned Families for A.T.V. Safety, said, "A.T.V.'s have been killing and maiming for years."

Source: *New York Times,* November 24, 2009 (by Leslie Wayne)

It is very rare to see a felony prosecution for corporate killings. One of the signal powers of corporations is their ability to influence the law and culture so that their most heinous acts are not considered criminal. Knowingly addicting millions of children to a deadly habit? Not a crime. Collaborate with military regimes and destroy lives and livelihoods in poor countries? Not a crime. Endanger that planet with greenhouse gas pollution, and then mobilize politically to block emergency efforts to save the Earth? Not a (corporate) crime.

Source: *Multinational Monitor*, June 30, 2009

"Even as drug makers promise to support Washington's health care overhaul by shaving $8 billion a year off the nation's drug costs, after the legislation takes effect, the industry has been raising its prices at the fastest rate in years.

"In the last year, the industry has raised the wholesale prices of brand-name prescription drugs by about 9 percent, according to industry analysts. That will add more than $10 billion to the nation's drug bill, which is on track to exceed $300 billion this year. By at least one analysis, it is the highest annual rate of inflation for drug prices since 1992."

Moreover, the *New York Times* adds, this uptick goes against the general economic flow given that the Consumer Price Index has dropped 1.3 percent since last year.

Such a sudden climb in prices is not unexpected, explains Stephen W. Schondelmeyer, a professor of pharmaceutical economics at the University of Minnesota. He stated, "When we have major legislation anticipated, we see a run-up in price-increases."

Looking historically, Joseph P. Newhouse, a Harvard health economist, pointed to the same price boosts for medicines that occurred when Medicare added drug benefits. In 2006, at the time the new program was being instated, Newhouse said that in order to "maximize their profits," pharmaceutical firms ratcheted up their prices by "the widest margin in a half-dozen years."

Source: *New York Times*, November 16, 2009 (by Duff Wilson)

Comment: The drug companies receive tax credits from the U.S. Treasury. They also get free research and development, resulting in clinically tested drugs, by the National Institutes of Health (NIH), which provides licenses to selected drug companies royalty free. There are no reasonable price restraints to protect patients. These massive giveaways are called CRADA (Cooperative Research and Development Agreement) agreements.

* * *

"From the edges of the Thames River in New London, Connecticut, Michael Cristofaro surveyed the empty acres where his parents' neighborhood had stood, before it became the crux of an epic battle over eminent domain.

"'Look what they did,' Mr. Cristofaro said. 'They stole our home for economic development. It was all for Pfizer, and now they get up and walk away.'

"That sentiment has been echoing around New London since Monday, when Pfizer, the giant drug company, announced it would leave the city just eight years after its arrival [which had] led to a debate about urban development that rumbled through the United States Supreme Court, and reset the boundaries for governments to seize private land for commercial use."

Pfizer had first been lured to this area in Connecticut as a site for its research unit headquarters by a big basket of financial incentives offered by the government, the *New York Times* reported. These included the waiving of four-fifths of the corporation's property taxes for the first decade of its stay.

To sweeten the deal, the government exercised eminent domain to seize properties on land that was needed for facilities, an action resisted by local residents in a case that ended up in the U.S. Supreme Court. The court ruled [in *Kelo v. New London*] that the state could take private property and hand it to developers when the property was to be used in a way that would "bolster the local economy."

Still, some justices were not happy with this decision. Justice Thomas opined that the New London's plan was "a costly urban-renewal project whose stated purpose is a vague promise of new jobs and increased tax revenue, but which is also suspiciously agreeable to the Pfizer Corporation."

Winning its case, Pfizer opened the headquarters, which covered 750,000 square foot and cost $294 million, in 2001.

Recently, however, the drug company has decided to abandon the facility, moving its unit to another Pfizer site, this time in Groton, and taking 1,400 jobs with it.

In place of the thriving research unit would be a vacant, large office complex, the city's biggest, and barren land from which the houses were removed in preparation for further developments, such as a hotel and stores, which never came.

Many local residents now see "Pfizer as a corporate

carpetbagger that took public money, in the form of big tax breaks, and now wants to run."

Source: *New York Times*, November 14, 2009 (by Patrick McGeehan)

Comment: The conservative attorney at the Institute for Justice, Scott G. Bullock, who represented the homeowners in the case, said of Pfizer's exit: "It really shows the folly of these plans that use massive corporate welfare and abuse eminent domain for private development."

* * *

"The number of Americans who lived in households that lacked consistent access to adequate food soared last year, to 49 million, the highest since the government began tracking what it calls 'food insecurity' 14 years ago, the Department of Agriculture reported Monday.

"The increase of 13 million Americans was much larger than even the most pessimistic observers of hunger trends had expected and cast an alarming light on the daily hardships caused by the recession's punishing effect on jobs and wages."

Analysts looking at these figures, according to the *Times*, attributed this increase largely to unemployment. At the end of 2007 unemployment stood at 4.9 percent of able-bodied workers; a year later, it has lifted to 7.2 percent, and now it's gone even higher, up to 10.2 percent. Add to that, experts continue, the rising food prices, and it's no surprise that the number of people going on food stamps is at record highs. Presently, there are 36 million Americans getting this aid, "an increase of nearly 40 percent from two years ago."

Source: *New York Times*, November 17, 2009 (by Jason DeParle)

Comment: The combination of Wall Street collapsing the economy with high unemployment and underemployment and a federal minimum wage of $7.25 per hour, which, if it had been adjusted for inflation from 1968, would now be $10 per hour, leaves the world's greatest bread basket country ever unwilling to eradicate the scourge of hunger and malnutrition among its people.

* * *

"On November 6, President Obama signed the Worker, Homeownership and Business Assistance Act of 2009 into law, extending unemployment benefits by 20 weeks and renewing the first-time homebuyer tax credit until next April.

"But tucked inside the law was another prize: a tax break that lets big companies offset losses incurred in 2008 and 2009 against profits booked as far back as 2004. The tax cuts will generate corporate refunds or relief worth about $33 billion, according to an administration estimate. ... The only companies that can't participate are Fannie Mae and Freddie Mac and any institution that took money under the Troubled Asset Relief Program.

"This is getting to be a habit," continues Gretchen Morgenson in the *New York Times*, "companies that participated on the upside and are now reaping rewards from the taxpayers on the downside. ... Dropping helicopter money on the home builders—the folks who massively overbuilt in community after community—seems decidedly less urgent (unless you are one of these companies, of course). Given that the supply of housing far outstrips demand, it is unlikely that these companies will use these tax breaks to hire workers."

Morgenson quotes Ivy Zelman, chief executive at research firm Zelman & Associates, who says, "I am surprised that home builders are getting hundreds of millions of dollars, given that many have very strong balance sheets." Zelman elaborated on this thought in these words, "We question the public policy decision to gift home builders with capital that many will not use to create jobs, since they admit that job growth will be dependent not on capital, but on improving demand."

Morgenson goes on to show the truth of Zelman's words concerning how many of these companies already possess substantial financial reserves, noting, for instance, that Pulte Homes, which is looking at a $450 million refund from this new law, already is sitting on $1.5 billion in cash and cash equivalents.

Representative Lloyd Doggett, a Texas Democrat, is one of the few legislators that has come out against this tax break, which he thinks is ill-advised, given there is little likelihood the recipients of the government's largesse will apply the money to job creation. He labels the tax break "a total windfall" for the lucky firms.

As might have been predicted, a good deal of lobbying money went into supporting this bill. Records show that Lennar spent $240,000; companies connected to Hovnanian Enterprises shelled out $222,000; and the aforementioned Pulte Homes ponied up $210,000 this year to push the legislation.

From their point of view, that was money well spent. For its $210,000, Pulte will get $450 million in refunds, while Hovnanian, having spent $222,000, is looking at as much as a $275 million tax return.

The taxpayers, meanwhile, as the author sardonically ends, are left holding a bag, which "gets bigger and bigger."

Source: *New York Times*, November 15, 2009 (by Gretchen Morgenson)

Comment: All this recalls the words of the Oklahoma sage, Will Rogers, who said: "Congress is the best money can buy."

* * *

"Goldman Sachs announced Tuesday that it would spend $500 million to help small businesses as part of a program offering education, mentoring and access to capital to 10,000 firms. ...

"Goldman's initiative comes as it tries to fight public perceptions of the firm as a greedy titan that benefited greatly from the government's extraordinary efforts to revive Wall Street but has done little to ease the ongoing pain on Main Street." It has also not helped the company's image, according to the *New York Times*, that, after the government bailout, it is now notching up record profits, and is about to ladle out big executive payments, with a mind-boggling $16.7 billion bonus package just for the first three quarters, easily topping the $11.4 billion that the company gave out in 2008.

Goldman's chief executive, Lloyd Blankfein, attempted to mollify the angry public, and those in the legislature who have expressed disgust with these supersized bonuses, by publicly apologizing for its part in the country's financial meltdown. According to Bloomberg News, he stated, "We participated in things that were clearly wrong and .... we apologize."

Source: *New York Times*, November 4, 2009 (by Tomoeh Murakami Tse)

Comment: How easy the hyper-rich escape! Wall Street devastates workers, consumers, pensions, savers and investors, is bailed out by taxpayers, and there is relief in a verbal apology and a snippet of $500 million (probably deductible) for 10,000 firms, which breaks out to $50,000 per firm, assuming no overhead expenses.

* * *

"A widely prescribed and expensive cholesterol drug is not as effective as niacin, a cheap vitamin, in helping to unclog coronary arteries in people already taking statins, the standard medicines used to lower cholesterol, according to a new study.

"The research, which appears Monday in the *New England Journal of Medicine*, is sending rumbles through the medical community because it is the third recent study to raise questions about the effectiveness of Zetia and its sister drug, Vytorin, highly profitable pharmaceuticals made by Merck & Co.

"'This is the third strike,' said Steven Nissen, chairman of cardiovascular medicine at the Cleveland Clinic. 'The studies are telling us that it doesn't appear to produce benefits. This is a drug used by millions of Americans, a very big seller, in a healthcare system where costs are a major issue.'"

The *New York Times* lays out that, globally, the drug had $4.56 billion in sales last year, with U.S. prescriptions reaching above 29 million.

Although Merck executives claim the drug is still valuable, and it has been shown to cut cholesterol, though it is of little help in warding off heart attacks and stroke or reducing cardiovascular problems, this is not the first time it has come under fire.

Last year, research indicated that Zetia did nothing to lower arterial plaque for patients already taking the much cheaper statins. Indeed, Merck itself released this study after holding back its publication for two years. This inordinate delay was at the heart of class action lawsuit, which alleged "Merck intentionally withheld unfavorable results of a clinical trial. The company paid $41.5 million in August to settle the claims."

Next up was another damaging report, which came out last year, and found that the affected who took Zetia and Vytoria had a greater risk of contracting cancer than did those who were only on statins.

Harlan Krumholz, a Yale University cardiologist, called the research "unnerving," and added, "The accumulating evidence isn't giving you any confidence. This is a very expensive drug being used without any strong evidence that it's benefiting patients."

Source: *New York Times*, November 18, 2009 (by Lyndsey Layton)

Comment: In recent years, so many heavy selling drugs have been shown either to be ineffective or to produce serious side effects. A painkiller, Vioxx, produced tens of thousands of heart attacks, for example. Who's minding the store, here? Who stands for the victims besides some plaintiff lawyers?

* * *

On February 27, 2008, Sidney M. Wolfe M.D. and Director of Public Citizen's Health Research Group warned Congress about the problems with the Food and Drug Administration (FDA) Center for Drug Evaluation and Research (CDER) and the Prescription Drug User Fee Act (PDUFA). Doctor Wolfe noted that an analysis of serious post-PDUFA mistakes made by CDER in approving a number of drugs that had evidence prior to approval of bright red warning signs illustrates the problem of CDER funding by industry:

Duract (bromfenac): The FDA Medical Officer reviewing bromfenac sodium, the 20th nonsteroidal anti-inflammatory drug (NSAID) approved in the United States, unsuccessfully advocated a black box warning label as a condition of approval because, "The review of the 'liver' laboratory data from the submission shows that bromfenac sodium causes hepatocellular damage to a greater degree than other NSAIDs". After at least 4 deaths and 8 liver transplants, bromfenac sodium was removed from the market.

Posicor (mibefradil): Data from congestive heart failure trials presented at a FDA Advisory Committee meeting on whether or not to approve mibefradil suggested that more patients treated with the drug died of sudden deaths than those taking placebo. Several committee members voted against approval. The drug, the ninth calcium channel blocker approved in the United States, has since been removed from the market because of life-threatening arrhythmias from drug interactions.

Rezulin (troglitazone): The 11th drug for diabetes in the United States, was approved even though 1.9 percent of patients in the pre-marketing trials, 54 percent of whom had taken the drug for at least 6 months, had liver function test results greater than 3 times the upper limit of normal, and 0.4 percent and 0.2 percent had 10-fold and 20-fold elevations, respectively. Well before it was removed from the market, troglitazone had already been associated with a minimum of 43 cases of liver failure, including 28 deaths.

Trovan (trovafloxacin): Trovafloxacin was approved by the FDA in 1997. Like Duract, there was also clear evidence of liver damage caused by Trovan in animals and in humans before the drug was approved in December 1997. In one pre-approval study in which the drug was used to treat prostatitis, 10 percent of the men (14 out of 140) given the drug developed evidence of liver toxicity. With 8 other drugs in this fluoroquinolone antibiotic family available in the U.S., as well as dozens of other safer and equally or more effective drugs for infections, the removal of Trovan from the market by the FDA would not have deprived doctors or patients of a drug that could possibly be considered indispensable. Instead of banning Trovan in 1999, as was done everywhere else in the world, the FDA chose to "limit" its use in the United States to patients who were either hospitalized or in nursing homes. At the time of our petition in 1999 to ban the drug, there were 8 cases of liver failure, including 5 deaths and 3 liver transplants. There were, as of December 31, 2004, a total of 58 cases of liver failure, including 29 deaths and 9 people requiring liver transplants. This is especially alarming since for the past several years there were a total of only 350,000 prescriptions filled in the U.S. (from April 2002 through February 2005). As sales waned following the 1999 market withdrawal in Europe but more and more cases of liver failure and death occurred, Pfizer quietly discontinued making the drug in 2002. However, during the latest year for which U.S. sales data are available, there were still 18,000 prescriptions filled in the U.S. (March 2004 through February 2005), long after Pfizer stopped manufacturing the drug.

Lotronex (alosetron): Seven cases of life-threatening ischemic colitis occurred in clinical trials for this drug with marginal benefits in treating the diarrhea variety of irritable bowel syndrome. Within 6 months of marketing an additional 16 cases had occurred....

Source: Dr. Sidney M. Wolfe's Congressional Testimony on FDA Deficiencies, February 27, 2008, Congressional Agriculture-FDA Appropriations SubCommittee Hearing on Drug Safety

* * *

When you heat up water, the first stage it goes through in becoming a gas is nucleate boiling. This is when only the surface of the water is hot and from it are emerging bubbles. I calculate that after reading about such corporate abuses as companies blocking scientists from learning about the effect of their genetically altered seeds, Pfizer abandoning its headquarters in a town after it had benefited from big tax breaks and forced people to give up their homes so it could locate there, and how banks are ripping off consumers, you are at this first stage, bubbles of rage emerging from your surface.

* * *

"In the official record of the historic House debate on overhauling health care, the speeches of many lawmakers echo with similarities. Often, that was no accident.

"Statements by more than a dozen lawmakers were ghostwritten, in whole or in part, by Washington lobbyists working for Genetech, one of the world's largest biotechnology companies.

"E-mail messages obtained by *The New York Times* show that the lobbyists drafted one statement for Democrats and another for Republicans."

Moreover, as the *Times* discovered, Genetech lobbyists managed to get these industry-ghosted remarks printed in the *Congressional Record,* presented as if they were original thoughts of the varied Congress members.

According to Genetech, it had good representation on both sides of the aisle with 22 Republicans and 20 Democrats using some of its talking points.

This was not a particularly remarkable feat according to a lobbyist close to the firm, who noted, "This happens all the time. There was nothing nefarious about it."

Source: *New York Times*, November 15, 2009 (by Robert Pear)

Comment: Taxpayers pay $3.5 billion to keep 535 members of the House and Senate comfortable and serviced by senior staff making between $100,000 and $200,000 a year, yet many let big corporations ghostwrite their public statements without disclosing this practice. I guess the ghostwriting Senators and Representatives don't think this is any big deal since the corporatists write many of the laws they pass in the first place. You'd think that at least our lawmakers would give us footnotes for attribution!

* * *

"A ray of sunlight broke through the Washington fog last week when Neil M. Barofsky, special inspector general for the Troubled Asset Relief Program (TARP), published his office's report on the government bailout last year of the American International Group.

"It's must reading for any taxpayer hoping to understand why the $182 billion "rescue" of what was once the world's largest insurer still ranks as the most troubling episode of the financial disaster.

"Many in Washington want to give more regulatory power to the Federal Reserve Board, the banking regulator that orchestrated the AIG bailout. Through this prism, the actions taken by Treasury Secretary Timothy F. Geithner, who was president of the Federal Reserve Bank of New York at the time, grow curious-er and curious-er."

Gretchen Morgenson, who made these statements in the *New York Times,* further noted that the "Fed failed to develop a workable rescue plan when AIG" was going down for the count, because it lacked money to fulfill various insurance contracts that had come due. The report argues that this was the time the Fed should have exacted concessions from the rich partners to whom AIG owed a payoff.

After all, according to the report, if AIG had defaulted, these partners would have received little compensation, so the Fed could have bargained from this position, rather than acting as it did and handing "AIG's counterparties 100 cents on the dollar." Large firms such as Goldman Sachs, Merrill Lynch, Societe Generale and other big banks were getting full recompense for their contracts while others, less favored, had to take "fire-sale prices."

In the report, Barofsky says that if the Fed was really protecting our interests, it would have forced the banks to accept a "haircut," that is a "steep discount," rather than giving them, in direct government money and in money already paid by AIG, a whopping "$62 billion for the contracts, which the report describes as 'far above their market value at the time.'"

Source: *New York Times*, November 22, 2009 (by Gretchen Morgenson)

Comment: This report describes what people mean when they say Washington has become corporate occupied territory—a corporate state where big business controls and turns government against its people. Think of what these giveaways could have built, such as schools, community clinics, modern public transit, safer drinking water and sewage treatment systems in your region. Think also how zero was your right to participate in the process leading to the bailout, even through your supine Congress, which had no problem with zeroing itself out of any real engagement. Finally, remember that phrase "equal under the law," just how equal are individual citizens as compared with giant corporations.

* * *

"When Senator Max Baucus (D.-Mont) this summer proposed a $4 billion tax on medical-device firms to help offset to cost of health-care reforms, an unusual mix of lawmakers joined in a chorus of protest."

Joining arms were Senator John F. Kerry (D.-Mass), Northeastern liberal, and Representative F. James Sensenbrenner (R.-Wis), a Midwestern conservative, according to this *Times* report. In Kerry's words, this tax would be hurting companies who are trying to create "new technology that saves lives and money" while Sensenbrenner claimed that through this tax the government would be damaging the economy.

It could be this strange alliance had its roots in an interesting parallel between the two men, as the *Times* writers suggest. Both have "millions of dollars of family wealth invested over the years in the companies that make medical devices."

The case is striking but no longer unusual in Washington, where our representatives are increasingly stock owners as well. This puts them more frequently in the position of making laws that may affect companies in which they hold investments. And this certainly suggests that their judgment may be clouded by concern for their own portfolios.

Source: *Washington Post*, November 23, 2009 (by Robert

O'Harrow, Jr., Kimberly Kindy and Dan Keating)

Comment: Such investments by members of Congress are legal. After all, Congress is a law unto itself; it can and does make laws for itself, as the above authors note: "On Wall Street and in federal agencies, the suggestion of a conflict is often the basis for an investigation."

* * *

"Ben Stein is an excellent independent business columnist for the *Sunday New York Times*. He is a lawyer, writer, actor and economist (ebiz@nytimes.com). On April 19, 2009, he wrote the following:

"I'd like to bring up one more little bijou about the economic crisis. I read that Lawrence H. Summers—wonderful guy, fine economist, former Harvard president, high-ranking economic adviser to Mr. Obama—was paid about $5 million last year by a large hedge fund, D.E. Shaw. Some other high-ranking Obama advisers were also fantastically well paid by the finance sector."

This is no novelty, Stein continues, seeing as, for example, the last Treasury secretary Henry M. Paulson Jr., had been the head of Goldman Sachs, a company that had royally compensated him hundreds of millions of dollars.

The problem, Stein notes, is that it's impossible to imagine that anyone, such as Summers or Paulson, "who has had a taste of honey from Wall Street on that scale will ever really crack the whip on Wall Street." And, therein, lies the problems with our government's attempts at financial regulation.

Source: *Sunday New York Times*, April 19, 2009 (by Ben Stein)

Bear Stearns and Lehman Brothers paid their executives largely in stock and that stock lost most or all of its value when those companies collapsed," writes Louise Story in the *New York Times*.

She goes on, "Many people on Wall Street say these examples help make the case that pay incentives were not what caused executives at these fallen firms to take excessive risks."

The truth of this proposition has been questioned by three Harvard professors, who argue that the top executives at these firms did not lose it all when their firms tanked.

While these corporate offices did see "$900 million in their stock holdings" disappear as their firms failed, this only seems like a complete wipeout if one ignores the execs' previous vast accumulation of bonuses, pay and cashed-in stock.

Looking at these monies, the professors note that Lehman saw its top five officers taking home $1 billion between 2000 and 2008; while Bear's top five did even better, scoring over $1.4 billion.

The Harvard study can be viewed on the website of the Program on Corporate Governance at Harvard Law School.

Source: *New York Times*, November 23, 2009 (by Louise Story)

Comment: Remember the old observation about the captain going down with his ship, as did the skipper of the Titanic? Not these Wall St. bosses. They jump ship and skip lucratively to the bank.

* * *

"The expansion of global trade may enrich the United States, as economists say, but it has overwhelmed this manufacturing area beside the Blue Ridge Mountains.

"The region has lost more of its jobs to international competition than just about anywhere else in the nation, according to federal trade assistance statistics, as textile mills have closed, furniture factories have dwindled and even the fiber-optic plants have undergone mass layoffs. The unemployment rate is one of the highest in the nation—about 15 percent.

"'Our stitching was perfection,' said Geraldine Ritch, 62, whose $15 an hour job sewing leather in a furniture factory was cut last year. 'So I never thought we'd lose our jobs to China. But we did. We *did*. Now what is everyone supposed to do?'"

With national unemployment rocketing upward, hitting 10

percent in October 2009, Peter Whoriskey notes in this *New York Times* piece, more and more people are questioning the free trade stance that has brought about manufacturing job losses like those that have been experienced in this region.

Displaced workers were supposed to be taken care of by a national retraining program, dubbed Trade Adjustment Assistance, which has a $1 billion annual budget, but Whoriskey's interviews "with a few dozen people here show, much of the damage to the affected workers is not so easily mended."

One of the area's legislative representatives, Patrick T. McHenry (R.-NC), lays the problem at China's doorstep, saying "Our unemployment problem began when China entered the world market full force." Admittedly, though, it was America's emphasis on free trade that left the country open to Chinese imports.

Source: *Washington Post*, November 10, 2009 (by Peter Whoriskey)

Comment: So-called "free trade" is not possible with dictatorships that determine key costs of production by outlawing independent trade unions, allowing pollution and bribes to thrive, holding down wages to under a $1.00 an hour while workers labor under the daily lash with modern capital equipment. U.S. workers cannot compete with these absolute advantages in authoritarian regimes like that of China. Also, "free trade" is supposed to be win-win for both parties. Well, the U.S. has registered burgeoning trade deficits for 32 years straight and has gone from being the world's leading creditor in 1980 to the world's leading debtor today. "Free traders" who run our government and corporate suites, now under the WTO and NAFTA, are oblivious to evidence. That is how a secular religion acts.

* * *

A Victory. A *Times* story states, "J.P. Morgan Securities will forfeit hundreds of millions of dollars in fees on derivatives contracts that it sold an Alabama county, under a settlement announced Wednesday that could offer hope to other governments staggering under similar deals.

"The Securities and Exchange Commission charged in a lawsuit on Wednesday that J.P. Morgan had made unlawful payments to friends of Jefferson County's commissioners in a scheme to win lucrative business from the county to sell bonds and trade in derivatives."

Two former J.P. Morgan employees were also mentioned in the suit, one of whom had already put in time in the big house "for manipulating similar bond deals in Philadelphia."

While J.P. Morgan didn't admit to any wrongdoing, it is paying a pretty penny to settle the suit, coughing up "a $25 million penalty to the commission and $50 million to the county." That doesn't include its agreement to withdraw a claim that Jefferson County pay $647 million in termination fees on derivatives. Perhaps in light of this, J.P. Morgan has now "discontinued its business of trading in derivatives with states and local governments."

Source: *New York Times*, November 5, 2009 (by Mary Williams Walsh)

Comment: Given the whopping money grabs involved, there just are nowhere near enough federal cops on the corporate crime beats. Corporate crime enforcement could be a profit-center for law and order.

* * *

"As many as 25 percent of American farmers growing genetically engineered corn are no longer complying with federal rules intending to maintain the resistance of the crops to damage from insects, according to a report Thursday from an advocacy group [the Center for Science in the Public Interest]."

This *Times* piece by Andrew Pollack quotes the advocacy group's report, which notes, "The increase in farmers skirting the rules, from fewer than 10 percent a few years ago, raises the risk that insects will develop resistance to the toxins in the corn that are meant to kill them."

BT corn, which the report is highlighting, is a crop that has been genetically modified so that it emits pest-killing toxins. The use of this corn is widespread, with 49 million acres of BT corn planted in 2008, which is 57 percent of U.S. corn acreage.

Up to now, bugs have not become resistant to the corn's poisons, which, if it happened, would pose a real danger because then insects would not only be able to devour BT corn without the toxins being an obstacle, but could also feast on the non-BT corn of organic farmers who utilize a bug spray that relies on the same insecticide toxins as those emitted by the corn.

In order to block insects from growing immunized, the "EPA requires farmers in the Corn Belt to plant 20 percent of their fields with non-BT corn to serve as a refuge for insects. The idea is that if an insect becomes impervious to the BT toxin, it is likely to mate with a nonresistant insect from the refuge, and the offspring would not be resistant." But, as the report indicates, a burgeoning number of farmers are ignoring these regulations, raising the specter of the emergence of super-bugs who are not affected by the BT toxins.

Source: *New York Times*, November 6, 2009 (by Andrew Pollack)

Comment: The above is just a glimmer of the complexities of bioengineered crops, along with migration of biotech seeds from one farm which contaminates an adjoining farm that refuses to buy such seeds, along with other questions raised by such groups as the Council for Responsible Genetics, started by MIT and Harvard scientists (see genewatch.org). Monsanto and its allies have blocked the government from requiring labeling of genetically modified food packages in supermarkets, a notification desired by over 90 percent of consumers.

* * *

"Wrestling with the slippery costs of Implants. When makers of heart defibrillators wanted Medicare to vastly expand the types of patients eligible to receive the devices, which can cost upward of $25,000, agency officials were skeptical. It was not clear how many of those patients would actually need a defibrillator, a device that can deliver a life-saving shock to restore a faltering heart to normal rhythm.

"So government and industry struck a deal back in 2004."

Barry Meier, writing in the *Times*, explained this deal. Medicare would double the number of those who could qualify for the defibrillator, pending a study, to be paid for by the medical device industry, which would determine which patients benefited from its installation.

Medicare is paying about $13 billion annually on the six highest-cost implanted devices. According to the Times, "Medicare underwrites more than half of the $4 billion the nation now spends annually on defibrillators, but the agency is no closer to knowing how many lives that big investment is saving."

Lo and behold, five years down the road, Medicare is paying for half the $4 billion the U.S. spends annually on defibulators, keeping its side of the bargain, but the industry seems to have dropped the ball on its end insofar as "the device companies did not finance the study beyond their initial $4 million commitment, and Medicare did not pick up the slack."

So, Medicare is paying for a device, without knowing whether this defibrillator is medically needed for the patient. "And doctors and patients have no way of knowing whether one producer's model performs better than a competitor's."

Source: *New York Times*, November 5, 2009 (by Barry Meier)

Comment: This is just one example of how corporations push Medicare around to their advantage and make sure Medicare is not aggressively pushing back against the industry's influence in Congress and the executive branch. Due to this, patients and taxpayers pay the price.

* * *

New York Times columnist Thomas L. Friedman offered this suggestive and dismaying commentary on his 2003 trip to Iraq. He begins, "I had arranged an appointment in the Green Zone with a member of the then-Iraqi Governing Council. Security was tight.

I was with my Iraqi translator, a middle-aged man who had once been a teacher. When we arrived at the council after a long walk, I showed my ID to two young uniformed U.S. soldiers.

"They told me to wait, went inside and out came a man wearing civilian clothes, one of those fishing vests and an Australian bush hat.

"He never properly identified himself, but it was obvious that he was a 'civilian contractor' from the logo on his shirt. When I tried to explain why we were there, he literally told me to shut my mouth until I was told to speak. Then he told my Iraqi translator to sit in the blistering heat while he escorted me—the American— inside to see if our Iraqi interviewee was available. I have to admit it: both my translator and I really wanted to just punch his lights out. But I kept thinking to myself: 'Who does this guy report to? If I get in his face and he comes after me, to whom do I complain?'"

This was not to be Friedman's only encounter with civilian contractors, such as guards, aid workers, and suppliers, who have come to play such a large part in our country's endeavors in Iraq and Afghanistan, including acting as providers of "'enhanced interrogations'—aka torture—of suspected terrorists at Abu Ghraib."

He discussed this trend with Allison Stanger, a professor of political economy at Middlebury College, who said the public is not aware of how many government functions are being taken up by the private sector. In her words, "Afghanistan and Iraq are our first contractors' wars, differing from previous interventions in their unprecedented reliance on the private sector for all aspects of their execution." She cited the Congressional Research Service, whose numbers indicate that in 2009 these private hirelings made up 48 percent of the Department of Defense workers in Iraq and 57 percent in Afghanistan.

These contractors fill any manner of roles, from training police to feeding and housing our troops, even providing security. But to Stanger, there is a clear danger on this reliance, for "when money and instructions change hands multiple times in a foreign country," she feels, it's not unlikely that lack of oversight will breed corruption and a tendency to pilfer from the public till. And this is not to mention the potential breeding of corporations, who become addicted to making money as government contractors in wars, and so will encourage foreign adventures as a way to keep the money flowing.

Source: *New York Times*, November 4, 2009 (by Thomas L. Friedman)

Comment: The above is just the tip of the iceberg. More investigations and audits by the Pentagon and the Congress will demonstrate the criminogenic nature of some of these big contracting companies as well as the excessive cost to the taxpayers. For example, the Army used to have its own cooks. Recently, Uncle Sam was charged by one of the big companies $240,000 for a single cook for a year to feed the soldiers in Iraq. Small wonder the company profits are huge.

* * *

"Free Trade Anyone? Despite a six-year effort to build trusted computer chips for military systems, the Pentagon now manufactures in secure facilities run by American companies only about *2 percent* of the more than $3.5 billion of integrated circuits bought annually for use in military gear."

This is hardly a happy situation, the *Times* notes, in that during times of military conflict we rely on weaponry and communication equipment, which will only function with these now foreign-made chips. So, with more and more work for the Pentagon being done at offshore semi-conductor manufacturing plants, the threat of hostiles sabotaging the chips or of shoddy workmanship making them inoperable at crucial moments, has become of great concern to the U.S. military.

Source: *New York Times*, October 27, 2009 (by John Markoff)

"Consider one of the actual news stories to emerge from Chicago of late: The city's decision to privatize its parking meters." So begins a hard-hitting story by Thomas Frank from the

Wall Street Journal, which continues, "Thanks to a deal finalized in 2008, Chicago's parking meters will be operated for the next 75 years by a group of investors put together by Morgan Stanley."

Taking the lead in our country's race to privatize government functions, the city already leased off the Chicago skyway, a South Side toll road, in 2005. This was followed the next year by the leasing of the city's downtown parking garages, which would have been succeeded by the privatization of Midway Airport, except the deal broke down.

As to the parking meter bargain, with good reason for its perpetrators, it was hurried through the city council, which was allowed only two days to look the compact over while the public generally knew nothing about it. Frank notes that Chicago's inspector general's opinion was: "No financial analysis was provided of the value of the parking meter system to the city. ... There was no public comment; no testimony from critics or experts; no presentation of recent studies."

One wonders whether it would have been approved if there were more public scrutiny, seeing as how, it was later learned, the privatizers only paid about half what the system was worth, according to the inspector general's report. A Chicago aldermen said even this was an underestimate of what the city lost, stating in the *Chicago Reader* that the meter system was worth at least quadruple its price. *The Reader*, after investigating the royal giveaway, concluded, "The taxpayers had been hosed."

But have Chicagoans appreciated the new service? Perhaps not, seeing as the cost of parking was "increased dramatically," so much so the meters broke down because they couldn't handle the amount of quarters they now had to accept from the boosted charges. In the end, "Chicagoans were furious."

Source: *Wall Street Journal*, November 4, 2009 (by Thomas Frank)

Comment: Privatization or more precisely, "corporatization" rarely is more efficient and in those rare instances where it is, the corporate bosses slash wages and benefits for their workers.

* * *

"Genetic Research Spurs Fight Over Patents Tied to the Body. The mapping of the human genome has created enticing possibilities for the early detection of grave diseases.

"Genetic research, however, has run headlong into a tricky legal issue: Should human genes ever be the subject of patent protection?" This is the opening question of a timely article by *Wall Street Journal* writer Nathan Koppel.

To be precise, currently it is not legal to patent a whole gene, but the government does allow the patenting of "genetic sequences that have been identified by researchers," Koppel writes.

This has become a legal issue due to a case underway in New York federal court, which concerns the patenting of the BRCA 1 and 2 genes. Possession of these genes has been correlated with a heightened risk of breast and ovarian cancers.

One can see that if the ability to identify this gene, and so diagnose a cancer risk, were patented, only the patent holder would be licensed to identify this gene thus determining if a patient is at risk.

This concern has also been a subject of discussion for a genetics-policy committee that works under the aegis of the Department of Health and Human Services, and which, in October, argued for the changing of the law that is now allowing the patenting of genetic sequences that are useful in diagnosis.

Dr. James, a genetics professor at the University of North Carolina School of Medicine and a member of the committee, stated that while it is worthwhile to encourage companies to study "genetic technologies," it is equally important not to put obstacles in front of patients seeking treatment.

Rep. Xavier Becerra (D.-CA) agrees with the committee's recommendation and will bring up legislation this year "that would ban the patent office from issuing new gene patents."

Source: *Wall Street Journal*, December 10, 2009 (by Nathan Koppel)

Comment: Businesses (e.g. the cotton industry) used to own slaves before the Civil War. Now corporations like Monsanto and Novartis are rushing to own our genetic material. There was hardly any public debate in Congress and silence during the major party presidential candidates' campaigns. As for flora and fauna, it's open season for corporate ownership of their genes.

* * *

"Too many of the leaders of the world's largest banks, brokerage houses and other financial powerhouses don't get it. They don't understand why the public is so angry at them and their paychecks. ... They don't see that they are widely seen as the ones who drove the world economy frighteningly close to the abyss of the second Great Depression."

After this powerful lead, the article goes on to quote Paul Volcker, former U.S. Federal Reserve chairman, who was speaking in London at the *Wall Street Journal* Future of Finance conference, and said to the gathered financiers, "You have not come anywhere close to responding with necessary vigor to the crisis we have had."

Still, the author continues, Americans are asking even more searching questions. The fundamental query is whether Wall Street is actually of any benefit to the broader economy. From Main Street, it would appear the stock market is all about rewarding big money players, come what may. These players are "pocketing the profits in good times and sticking the taxpayers with losses in bad times." On the other hand, this part of the financial system is not about making the economy sound or offering a good life and prospects to America's children.

Source: *Wall Street Jounal*, December 10, 2009 (by David Wessel)

"What Charges Lurk on the Phone Bill? In this episode, the Haggler spends several days tracking down the source of a gratuitous $8.67 charge. "'Hey Haggler,' you say, 'aren't there some real scandals out there to investigate? Have you nothing better to do with your time?'

"Not really. Because the Haggler is endlessly fascinated by the many ill-gotten fortunes in this country that are earned in tiny increments, usually buried in places that make them easy to overlook."

So begins a humorous and informative column by David Segal, writing as "The Haggler" in the *New York Times*. He has been spurred to write this particular piece by a letter he received from Trudi Coakley of New York City.

She told him that she was surprised to find on her Verizon phone bill an $8.67 charge for unknown services provided by Enhanced Billing Services, Inc. She was puzzled because she had "never signed up for" any service provided by the mysterious Enhanced. So she called, and her provider, who agreed she had been unnecessarily charged and had never requested anything from Enhanced, cancelled the service.

Even though this mistake was easily corrected, Coakley notes, "I believe posting charges for unsolicited services on my phone bill is sneaky and underhanded and perhaps even illegal." After all, how many harried or careless customers will overlook such an added charge and pay for something they didn't ask for and didn't need?

Source: *New York Times*, December 13, 2009 (by David Segal)

Comment: Computerized billing fraud and abuse is big business. For example, the Government Accountability Office of the Congress believes such abuses drain 10 percent of the health-care dollar every year, which in 2010 will be over $260 billion. The nation's expert on this subject says it could be higher and has written a book titled *License to Steal* by Professor Malcolm Sparrow, who teaches at Harvard.

* * *

Exxon Mobil Corporation plead guilty last week to violating a criminal provision of the Clean Water Act in connection with a spill of approximately 15,000 gallons of diesel oil into the Mystic River from Exxon Mobil's oil terminal in Everett, Massachusetts.

Exxon Mobil's negligent failure to provide adequate resources and oversight to the maintenance and operation of the Everett terminal was a direct cause of the spill.

As part of its plea agreement, Exxon Mobil will pay the maximum fine of $359,018, the clean-up costs of $179,634, and a community service payment of $5,640,982 to the North American Wetlands Conservation Act fund to be used to restore wetlands in Massachusetts.

Source: *Corporate Crime Reporter*, January 5, 2009

Siemens Aktiengesellschaft (Siemens AG), a German corporation and three of its subsidiaries pled guilty to violations of and charges related to the Foreign Corrupt Practices Act (FCPA)....

According to court documents, beginning in the mid-1990s, Siemens AG engaged in systematic efforts to falsify its corporate books and records and knowingly failed to implement and circumvent existing internal controls. ...

Siemens AG made payments totaling approximately $1.36 billion through various mechanisms.

Of this amount, approximately $554.5 million was paid for unknown purposes, including approximately $341 million in direct payments to business consultants. The remaining $805.8 million of this amount was intended in whole or in part as corrupt payments to foreign officials through the payment mechanisms, which included cash desks and slush funds.

"This pattern of bribery by Siemens was unprecedented in scale and geographic reach. The corruption involved more than $1.4 billion in bribes to government officials in Asia, Africa, Europe, the Middle East and the Americas," said Linda Chatman Thomsen, Director of the SEC's Division of Enforcement.

In connection with the cases brought by the Department of Justice, the SEC and the Munich Public Prosecutor's Office, Siemens AG will pay a combined total of more than $1.6 billion in fines, penalties and disgorgement of profits, including $800 million to U.S. authorities, making the combined U.S. penalties the largest monetary sanction ever imposed in a FCPA case since the act was passed by Congress in 1977.

Source: *Corporate Crime Reporter*, January 5, 2009

Leo Burnett Advertising Firm Pays United States $15.5 million to settle overbilling on army contract.

Teledyne Reynolds to pay $825,000 to resolve allegations it billed the Air Force for unallowable executive compensation.

Spartan Motors and its subsidiary, Spartan Chassis, will pay the United States $51.7 million to resolve allegations that it paid kickbacks to an employee of Force Protection Inc. to receive the subcontract to provide chassis for armored vehicles for the United States Military.

ExxonMobil will pay nearly $6.1 million in civil penalties for violating the terms of a 2005 court-approved Clean Air Act Agreement.

The owner and operator of two Miami medical clinics has pled guilty to defrauding the Medicare program in connection with a $5.3 million HIV infusion fraud scheme.

The Occupational Safety and Health Administration (OSHA) has reached an agreement with Cintas Inc. that the company will pay almost $3 million in penalties to resolve six cases currently pending before the Occupational Safety and Health Review Commission.

Source: *Corporate Crime Reporter*, January 12, 2009

Comment: These settlements or guilty pleas by corporate criminals occur week after week, but federal investigators and law enforcement officials know that with greater enforcement budgets and prosecutions, a far larger number of corporate criminals could be caught. The fines and disgorgement of profits could far, far exceed the government's enforcement budget. The sums could be so large they could discernibly reduce the federal deficit and deter further corporate crime and fraud. Congress knows this but deliberately keeps these corporate crime enforcement budgets small. For example, there are around 80 attorneys in the Justice Department's Environmental Crimes Division. There are more lawyers than that defending corporate polluters in just one giant corporate law firm.

* * *

The following is taken from "Interview with Patrick Burns, Communications Director, Taxpayers Against Fraud, Washington, D.C."

"The total recovery under some portion of the False Claims Act is going to be well over $4 billion this year.

"The first point to make about the Civil Division [of the Justice Department] is that as far as I can tell, they are completely apolitical. The Civil Division lawyers are straight shooting, hardworking folks. My only criticism is that the Civil Division has not been given the resources to do the job. And that is not the quality—it's the quantity. We just need more people at the Civil Division. We have a situation in which we have a massive swamp of fraud in this country. The swamp is getting bigger for a simple reason.

"Iraq and Afghanistan have geared up as massive frauds. Katrina slammed into Louisiana. And there have been massive frauds down there. Medicare Part D started up. Now we have the Toxic Asset Recovery Program. We have the fraud in and around the mortgage business. ... We are trying to drain a swamp with a garden hose.

"There are only about 100 cases a year being moved in the False Claims Act arena. And it hasn't gone up—or down. That's as many cases that can run through the pipe. And that's a problem. If you have an expanding swamp of fraud, you need to expand the pipe you are using to drain the swamp with. And that's where Congress and the White House have fallen down.

"What has hammered America to its knees over the past decade has been fraud—massive fraud. Jaw-dropping levels of fraud from Bernie Madoff to Bank of America. It's just astounding.

"I'm not sure we are going to be able to change the culture of big business unless we fully fund the fraud fighters at the U.S. Department of Justice. We have great people there. Let's triple the size of the Civil Division. That's where I would start.

"We're learning that if you find a fraud in Washington state, it's probably a fraud across the country. Even if it's a fraud in a class of drugs or medical devices or a kind of hospital fraud, it's probably manifest throughout the nation. And these business plan frauds are a little bit like corporate cancer that reach across the country. ...

"Ninety-five percent of the companies that made hip and knee devices were nailed for fraud in one fell swoop by the U.S. Department of Justice."

Source: *Corporate Crime Reporter*, May 18, 2009

According to the *New York Times*, "Three federal agencies and a loose consortium of state attorneys general have for several years been gathering evidence of what appears to be collusion among the banks and other companies that have helped state and local governments take approximately $400 billion worth of municipal notes and bonds to market each year." The evidence of this wrongdoing, which appears in emails, "taped phone conversations and other court documents," indicates that, in the manner of a classic cartel, there was no competition for the business, which was divvied up between the companies, thus adding to the price of marketing the notes and bonds as well as violating federal law. On top of this, bribery seems to have played a role in the placement of the government paper in that "questionable payments and campaign contributions [were made by banks] to local officials who could steer them business."

And, the *Times* continues, this was hardly the case of a few rogue traders involved in shady practices, but "the way an entire market has operated for years."

Charles Anderson, retired manager of tax-exempt bond field operations for the Internal Revenue Service, put it in a nutshell, "Pay-to-play in the municipal bond market is epidemic."

Source: *New York Times*, January 9, 2009 (by Mary Williams Walsh)

Comment: This widespread racket has been going on for years and it is so ingrained that intermittent prosecutions, large conviction or settlements do not seem to stem the large tidal wave of graft.

* * *

"Justice Department officials rolled out their second-largest price-fixing settlement, a $585 million penalty shared by three companies that make high-tech liquid crystal display panels for computer monitors, television and cell phones."

Source: *Washington Post*, January 2, 2009 (by Carrie Johnson)

Comment: That is, the second largest settlement since the 2008 Presidential elections in November 2008. This fine is about 50 percent of the Securities and Exchange Commission's annual budget.

* * *

American pharmaceutical giant Eli Lilly and Company will plead guilty and pay $1.415 billion for promoting its drug Zyprexa for uses not approved by the Food and Drug Administration (FDA). Eli Lilly promoted Zyprexa for the treatment of agitation, aggression, hostility, dementia, Alzheimer's dementia, depression and generalized sleep disorder. (All unapproved uses by FDA.)

This resolution includes a criminal fine of $515 million, the largest ever in a health care case. ... Eli Lilly will also pay up to $800 million in a civil settlement with the federal government and the states.

The company also caused false claims for payment to be submitted to federal insurance programs such as Medicaid, TRICARE and the Federal Employee Health Benefits Program, none of which provided coverage for such off label uses.

Source: *Corporate Crime Reporter*, January 19, 2009

Comment: But how much did Eli fully take in while the profitable violations were going on?

* * *

United Health Group Inc., the nation's second largest health insurer, settled New York state charges that it engaged in a scheme to defraud consumers by manipulating reimbursement rates.

At the center of the scheme is Ingenix, Inc., a wholly-owned subsidiary of United, which is the nation's largest provider of health care billing information.

Under the agreement with United, the database of billing information operated by Ingenix will close.

United will pay $50 million to a qualified nonprofit organization that will establish a new, independent database to help determine fair out-of-network reimbursement rates for consumers throughout the United States.

"For the past ten years, American patients have suffered from unfair reimbursements for critical medical services due to a conflict-ridden system that has been owned, operated, and manipulated by the health insurance industry. This agreement marks the end of that flawed system," said New York Attorney General Andrew Cuomo. ... During these tough economic times, this agreement will keep hundreds of millions of dollars in the pockets of over one hundred million Americans.

Source: *Corporate Crime Reporter*, January 19, 2009

Comment: This case shows how much these corporate abusers win even when they lose. Fifty million dollars paid out but hundreds of millions of dollars kept over ten years.

* * *

"SouthernCare Inc. will pay the United States a total of $24.7 million to settle allegations that the Birmingham, Alabama-based company submitted false claims to the government for patients treated at its hospice facilities.

SouthernCare operates approximately 99 locations that provide hospice services in 15 states.

The government alleged that SouthernCare had submitted

false claims for hospice care for patients who were not eligible for such care.

The settlement results from two qui tam suits filed by two former SouthernCare employees, Tanya Rice and Nancy Romeo, on behalf of the United States. The False Claims Act authorizes private parties to file suit against those who defraud the United State and to receive a share of any recovery.

The United States will pay $4.9 million to the individuals who filed the actions against SouthernCare."

Source: *Corporate Crime Reporter*, January 19, 2009

A U.S. Army Criminal Investigations Division investigator has recommended changing the official manner [classification] of death for a soldier electrocuted while showering at his base in Iraq from "accidental" to "negligent homicide," according to an e-mail from the investigator obtained by CNN.

According to the CNN report, the investigator blames KBR, the largest U.S. contractor in Iraq, and two KBR supervisors for the incident, saying there is "credible information ... they failed to ensure that work was being done by qualified electricians and plumbers, and to inspect the work that was being conducted."

The 24-year-old Green Beret, Ryan Maseth, died in a shower at his base in Iraq.

His death was just one of many fatalities now believed to be linked to shoddy electrical work at U.S. bases managed by U.S. contractors, according to Pentagon sources.

Just after Maseth's electrocution, Pentagon officials estimated that about a dozen troops had been electrocuted in Iraq. But Pentagon officials now say at least 18 troops have been electrocuted since 2003—many due to faulty wiring and improper grounding, CNN reported.

Source: *Corporate Crime Reporter,* January 26, 2009

Comment: Ponder the impunity of DOD corporate contractors, and their escape from full responsibility for these fatalities.

* * *

"Charles Bolton, a Memphis-based financial services provider, pled guilty to a one-count information [accusation] charging him with conspiracy to defraud the Internal Revenue Service in connection with tax shelters marketed by the accounting firm Ernst & Young.

"The shelters purported to allow wealthy individuals to pay a percentage of their income in fees to Ernst & Young, the Bolton companies, and other participants in the transactions, rather than paying taxes to the IRS."

Source: *Corporate Crime Reporter*, January 26, 2009

Coke Sued for Fraudulent Claims on Obesity Promoting VitaminWater. Coke markets VitaminWater as a healthful alternative to soda by labeling its several flavors with such health buzz words as "defense," "rescue," "energy," and "endurance."

The company makes a wide range of dramatic claims, including that its drinks variously reduce the risk of chronic disease, reduce the risk of eye disease, promote healthy joints, and support optimal immune function.

In fact, according to the Center for Science in the Public Interest (CSPI) nutritionists, the 33 grains of sugar in each bottle of VitaminWater do more to promote obesity, diabetes, and other health problems than the vitamins in the drinks do to perform the advertised benefits listed on the bottles.

VitaminWater contains between zero and one percent juice despite product names such as "endurance peach mango" and "focus kiwi strawberry."

"VitaminWater is Coke's attempt to dress up soda in a physician's white coat. Underneath, it's still sugar water, albeit sugar water that costs about ten bucks a gallon," said CSPI litigation director, Steve Gardner.

"My advice to consumers is to get your vitamins from real food," said CSPI executive director Michael F. Jacobson. "If you have reason to believe you have a shortcoming of one vitamin or another, perhaps take an inexpensive supplement. But don't seek out your vitamins in sugary soft drinks like Coke's VitaminWater."

Source: *Corporate Crime Reporter*, January 26, 2009

Mercury was found in nearly 50 percent of tested samples of commercial high fructose corn syrup (HFCS), according to a new article published in the scientific journal, *Environmental Health*.

A separate study by the Institute for Agriculture and Trade Policy (IATP) detected mercury in nearly one-third of 55 popular, brand-name food and beverage products where HFCS is the first or second highest labeled ingredient—including products by Quaker, Hershey's, Kraft and Smucker's.

HFCS use has skyrocketed in recent decades as the sweetener has replaced sugar in many processed foods.

HFCS is found in sweetened beverages, breads, cereals, breakfast bars, lunch meats, yogurts, soups and condiments. On average, Americans consume about 12 teaspoons per day of HFCS. Consumption by teenagers and other high consumers can be up to 80 percent above average levels.

"Mercury is toxic in all its forms," said IATP's David Wallinga, M.D., and a co-author in both studies. "Given how much high fructose corn syrup is consumed by children, it could be a significant additional source of mercury never before considered. We are calling for immediate changes by industry and the FDA to help stop this avoidable mercury contamination of the food supply."

Source: *Corporate Crime Reporter*, February 2, 2009

Patriot Coal Corporation, one of the largest coal mining companies in the United States, has agreed to pay a $6.5 million civil penalty to settle violations of the Clean Water Act. In addition, Patriot has agreed to extensive measures designed to ensure Clean Water Act compliance at its mines in West Virginia.

In a joint compliant filed concurrently with the consent decree, the United States and the State of West Virginia alleged that Patriot violated its Clean Water permits more than 1,400 times— representing over 22,000 days of violations between January 2003 and December 2007 at its mining complexes in West Virginia.

During this time, Patriot and its subsidiaries allegedly

discharged excess amount of metals, sediment, and other pollutants into dozens of rivers and streams in West Virginia. Excess discharges of these pollutants can significantly harm water quality and aquatic life in West Virginia's streams.

Source: *Corporate Crime Reporter*, February 9, 2009

UBS AG, Switzerland's largest bank, has entered into a deferred prosecution agreement on charges of conspiring to defraud the United States by impeding the Internal Revenue Service.

As part of the deferred prosecution agreement, UBS has further agreed to pay $780 million in fines, penalties, interest and restitution. Earlier today, the agreement was accepted in Ft. Lauderdale, Florida, by U.S. District Judge James I. Cohn.

The information also alleges that Swiss bankers routinely traveled to the United States to market Swiss bank secrecy to United States clients interested in attempting to evade United States income taxes. Court documents assert that, in 2004 alone, Swiss bankers allegedly traveled to the United States approximately 3,800 times to discuss their clients' Swiss bank accounts.

Source: *Corporate Crime Reporter*, February 23, 2009

Five billion in political contributions bought Wall Street Freedom from Regulation, Restraint, Report Finds.

The financial sector invested more than $5 billion to purchase political influence in Washington over the past decade, with as many as 3,000 lobbyists winning deregulation and other policy decisions that led directly to the current financial collapse, according to a 231-page report issued by Essential Information and the Consumer Education Foundation.

The report, *Sold Out: How Wall Street and Washington Betrayed America*, shows that, from 1998-2008, Wall Street investment firms, commercial banks, hedge funds, real estate companies and insurance conglomerates made $1.725 billion in political contributions and spent another $3.4 billion in lobbyists, a financial juggernaut aimed at undercutting federal regulation.

Nearly 3,000 officially registered federal lobbyists worked for the industry in 2007 alone. The report documents a dozen distinct deregulatory moves that, together, led to the financial meltdown. These include prohibitions on regulating financial derivatives; the repeal of regulatory barriers between commercial banks and investment banks; and federal refusal to act to stop predatory subprime lending."

"The report details, step-by-step, how Washington systemically sold out to Wall Street," says Harvey Rosenfield, president of the Consumer Education Foundation, a California-based non-profit organization. "Depression-era programs that would have prevented the financial meltdown that began last year were dismantled, and the warnings of those who foresaw disaster were drowned in an ocean of political money. Americans were betrayed, and we are paying a high price—trillions of dollars—for that betrayal."

"Congress and the Executive Branch," says Robert Weissman of Essential Information and the lead author of the report, "responded to the legal bribes from the financial sector, rolling back common-sense standards, barring honest regulators from issuing rules to address emerging problems and trashing enforcement efforts. The progressive erosion of regulatory restraining walls led to a flood of bad loans, and a tsunami of bad bets based on those bad loans. Now, there is wreckage across the financial landscape." For the entire report and list of the dozen key steps to financial meltdown, see wallstreetwatch.org.

Source: *Corporate Crime Reporter*, March 9, 2009

We Told You So. When Citibank and Travelers announced their merger in 1998—a marriage that could only be consummated if Glass-Steagall and related rules were repealed—my colleague Russell Mokhiber and I [Robert Weissman] wrote, "Expect to see lots of bad loans, bad investment decisions, teetering banks and tottering insurance companies, and a series of massive financial bailouts of new conglomerates judged "too big to fail."

We didn't envision exactly how the Citigroup and Wall Street debacle would play out, but we got the outline right. Our predictions echoed the warnings from consumer advocates.

Source: *Multinational Monitor*, March 12, 2009 (by Robert

Weissman)

Comment: When Barack Obama became President, with him in his first group photo after the election was Robert Rubin, the Treasury Secretary, architect of deregulation of the financial industry under Clinton and the co-head of Citigroup, who helped develop the bank's strategy for financial disaster that harmed so many innocent investors and homeowners and almost destroyed Citigroup. Were it not for a massive secret weekend bailout worked out by Rubin, Federal Reserve Chairman Ben Bernanke and Treasury Secretary (under Bush), Henry Paulson, Citigroup would have failed. President Obama selected another architect of Clinton's deregulation, former Secretary of the Treasury (after Rubin) Larry Summers as his chief economic advisor. There were no consumer advocates around Obama either at White House meetings or within his new Administration in this economic policy area.

* * *

Senator Bernie Sanders (I.-VT) last week introduced legislation that would make the Treasury Department identify and break up financial institutions that are "too big to fail."

"If an institution is too big to fail, it is too big to exist," Sanders said. "We should break them up so they are no longer in a position to bring down the entire economy. We should end the concentration of ownership that has resulted in just four huge financial institutions holding half the mortgages in America, controlling two-thirds of the credit cards, and amassing 40 percent of all deposits.

"One result of the burgeoning concentration of ownership has been outrageously high bank fees and interest rates for credit cards, mortgages and other financial products," Sanders said.

"No single financial institution should have holdings so extensive that its failure would cause catastrophic risk to millions of American jobs or to our nation's economic well-being. No single financial institution should have holdings so extensive that its failure could send the world economy into crisis," Sanders said. "We need to break up these institutions because they have done just tremendous damage to our economy."

Source: *Corporate Crime Reporter*, November 16, 2009

Comment: Wonderful bills are introduced in Congress with a descriptive press release. The vast majority are never heard from again, never even receiving a public Congressional hearing. One reason is that the people back home have no daily advocacy organization to push these bills toward enactment—even though they command large majorities of public opinion. Especially this one. It just shows that one or two big banks can overcome 100 million passive Americans, then move to use their taxes for bailout and gouge them as consumers. That's big time control.

* * *

Henry Morris and David Loglisci were indicted last week for bribery, corruption and other offenses related to a pay to play scheme operated out of the office of the New York State Comptroller.

The charges entail a web of corrupt acts for both political and personal gain." The state pension fund is the biggest pool of money in the State and the third largest public pension fund in the country, most recently valued at approximately $122 billion....

The New York State Controller is the sole trustee of the Fund, responsible for managing and investing the pension fund solely in the best interests of the over one million current and former State employees and their families.

From 2003 to 2006, Hank Morris was Comptroller, Alan Hevesi's top political advisor, and David Loglisci was the Chief Investment Officer in the Comptroller's Office. [Mr. Hevesi was forced to resign pursuant to an indictment by the District Attorney that led to a settlement].

"Mixing politics, self-dealing, kickbacks, and billions in taxpayer funds is nothing short of the perfect public integrity storm," said Attorney General Andrew Cuomo.

The indictment alleges that the process of selecting investments at the Fund—investments of billions of dollars—was skewed and corrupted to favor political associates, family and friends of

Morris and Loglisci, and other officials in the Office of the State Comptroller....

The indictment charges that Morris and others corrupted billions of dollars worth of [pension fund] investments from which they reaped more than $30 million in undisclosed fees, gifts, and bribes.

[The defendants have pled not guilty and are awaiting trial at this writing.] On April 16, 2010, the *New York Times* reported that "the investment firm founded by Steven L. Rattner, the politically connected financier who went on to lead President Obama's auto task force, has agreed to pay $12 million to settle allegations that it paid kickbacks to win lucrative business from the New York State Pension fund."

Source: *Corporate Crime Reporter*, March 23, 2009

The former senior vice president of City of Angels Medical Center pleaded guilty to paying illegal kickbacks to recruiters who referred homeless patients to the hospital, where they received unnecessary health services.

Dante Nicholson, 51, of Palmdalo, admitted paying illegal kickbacks as part of a scheme to defraud Medicare and Medi-Cal by recruiting homeless persons from the "Skid Row" district of downtown Los Angeles.

As part of the scheme, City of Angels entered into sham "consulting contracts intended to conceal the illegal kickbacks."

City of Angels billed Medicare and Medi-Cal for inpatient services to the recruited homeless beneficiaries, including those for home inpatient hospitalization that was not medically necessary.

Source: *Corporate Crime Reporter*, March 23, 2009

A new study released last week by the national consumer rights group Center for Justice & Democracy (CJD) finds that medical devices for the heart have caused thousands of needless injuries and deaths, yet patients currently have no legal recourse against reckless medical device manufacturers.

The release of the report, *Heart Sick—Hazardous Heart Devices and the Importance of Litigation*, comes one day before dozens of patients living with faulty medical devices head to Washington to urge Congress to restore their legal rights.

These rights were taken away by the U.S. Supreme Court last year in a case called *Riegel vs. Medtronic*.

That decision immunized negligent and irresponsible medical device companies whose defective devices injure or kill patients or force them to live knowing their device could fail at any moment. Legislation has currently been introduced in both Houses of Congress to fix this Supreme Court decision.

"This study tells a devastating tale of greed, cover-ups and reckless behavior by some companies that manufacture heart devices, such as pacemakers, defibrillators, heart valves and stents," said Joanne Doroshow, Executive Director of CJD. "Some of these devices were placed on the market without adequate testing. This has been with the acquiescence of the Food and Drug Administration, which has repeatedly been unable to properly oversee this hazardous industry."

Source: *Corporate Crime Reporter*, April 13, 2009

Comment: The Supreme Court referred to the clause in the Medical Device amendment to pre-empt state lawsuits, under common law, because the device received pre-market approval by the FDA. The reality is that corporate influence over the FDA has resulted in inadvisable approvals, absolute approvals, and does not recognize manufacturing defects in these products or other subsequent operating failures.

* * *

The PBS TV show *Frontline* last week aired its much awaited expose of foreign bribery—"Black Money."

Frontline reported that as the global financial downturn continues and pressure for profits increases on corporations across the world, a small group of lawyers in the U.S. Justice Department is pursuing an aggressive crackdown against an international business tactic—bribery—which the World Bank says amounts to as much as a trillion dollars a year in payments.

"Over the past two years, the U.S. government has collected almost a billion and a half dollars in fines in foreign bribery cases," said Mark Mendelsohn, the Department of Justice prosecutor in charge of more than 100 ongoing cases, one of which culminated in a record seven-year prison term for the former CEO of a subsidiary of the Halliburton Corp., and another which ended in a record $800 million fine against the German giant Siemens. "There's a whole world of conduct that rarely sees the light of day."

In "Black Money," *Frontline* correspondent Lowell Bergman investigates this shadowy side of international business, shedding light on multinational companies that have routinely made secret payments—often referred to as "black money"—to win billions in business.

"The thing about black money is you can claim it's being used for all kinds of things," the British reporter David Leigh tells Bergman. "You get pots of black money that nobody sees, nobody has to account for ... you can do anything you like with. Mostly what happens with black money is people steal it because they can."

Source: *Corporate Crime Reporter*, April 13, 2009.

Despite receiving requests by citizen groups for years, the Justice Department still has not asked Congress to establish a corporate crime data base and issue an annual report on corporate crime. The Department certainly has the authority to do this already, but it has claimed that it would need an appropriation from Congress for the budget.

It has been thirty years since the Department has undertaken a comprehensive study of the extent and cost of corporate crime in the United States. In a letter which I and my associates, Jim Donahue and Charles Cray, sent to Attorney General Eric Holder, we recounted the repeated requests and meetings but to no avail. The Justice Department never said no and never said yes.

The FBI oversees the Uniform Crime Reporting (UCR) Program which tracks certain categories of street crime from over 17,000 local and state law enforcement agencies. The UCR program's annual reports constitute a useful barometer of trends in street crime.

Our letter asserted that "an equivalent program should exist to collect and track information on various types of corporate crime and corporate law-breaking, including but not limited to antitrust and price-fixing, environmental crimes, financial crimes—including the various types of accounting fraud witnessed in recent years—overseas bribery, health care fraud, trade violations, labor and injuries and death, consumer fraud and tax fraud.

"We have written every administration since 1992, urging them to do this," Donahue said. "With today's technology, this effort will be easier than ever."

Cray said if the government can do it for street crime, it should be able to do it for corporate crime as well.

Aggregating the prevalence of corporate crime and other law-breaking detects trends elevates attention to compliance by federal agencies and provides support for adequate budgets, research and public alerts.

Source: *Corporate Crime Reporter*, April 6, 2009

Despite pledges by President Obama to protect federal whistle-blowers, the reality of retaliation inside the agencies remains unchanged, according to Public Employees for Environmental Responsibility (PEER).

Nor has the Obama administration ended Bush-era prosecutions of civil servants who blew the whistle.

Unlike issues such as the Freedom of Information Act where the Obama administration has announced new policies, there have been no new directives establishing a zero-tolerance policy against whistleblower harassment. ... The Obama administration could send an unmistakable signal by restoring whistleblowers to positions empowered to fix the problems for which they risked their careers.

Source: *Corporate Crime Reporter*, April 20, 2009

Northrop Grumman Corp., its subsidiary Northrop Grumman Space and Mission Systems Corp. and its predecessor TRW Inc., will pay the United States $325 million to resolve allegations made under the False Claims Act that Northrop provided and billed the National Reconnaissance Office (NRO) for defective microelectronic parts, known as Heterojunction Bipolar Transistors (HBTs).

The government's investigation in the HBT Action concluded that Northrop and TRW failed to properly test and qualify certain HBT's manufactured by TRW from 1992 to 2002. As a result, Northrop and TRW integrated into NRO satellite equipment certain defective HBTs.

The investigation also concluded that Northrop and TRW made misrepresentations about, and concealed certain material facts regarding the reliability of the HBTs....

The settlement resolves a Qui Tam or whistleblower lawsuit filed by Robert Ferro, PhD, an employee of the Aerospace Corporation.

The government investigated Dr. Ferro's allegations and intervened in the lawsuit against Northrop....

Under the agreement, Dr. Ferro will receive $48.75 million as his share of the recovery in the HBT action under the Qui Tam provisions of the False Claims Act.

Source: *Corporate Crime Reporter*, April 6, 2009

Lawsuits Filed Over KBR Iraq Burn Pits. There is a kind of leukemia called AML, acute myeloid leukemia. A large number of Iraq war vets have died in recent years of AMI. Why?

That's the question being asked by Elizabeth Burke. Burke is a partner at Burke O'Neil in Washington, DC. She's representing more than 70 former military personnel, contractors, and their survivors suing KBR.

The lawsuits allege that the giant Houston-based Iraqi contractor jeopardized the health and safety of American soldiers and contractors in Iraq and Afghanistan by burning vast quantities of unsorted waste in enormous open-air burn pits with no safety controls.

KBR is accused of allowing thick, noxious smoke — coming off

of flames sometimes colored blue or green by burning chemicals—
to hang over U.S. bases and camps across Iraq and Afghanistan
since 2004.

Round-the-clock hazardous emissions from the burn pits
allegedly caused serious respiratory illnesses, tumors and cancers
in the plaintiffs.

"US soldiers and other residents of the military bases and
camps have become seriously ill, been diagnosed with serious and
potentially fatal diseases and in some cases have died from the
physical injuries and diseases caused by the exposure to hazardous
smoke and fumes," the lawsuit alleged.

The burn pits are so large that tractors are used to push waste
onto them and the flames shoot hundreds of feet into the sky,
according to the lawsuits.

KBR allegedly burned waste such as biohazard materials,
human corpses, medical supplies, paints, solvents, asbestos, items
containing pesticides, animal corpses, tires, lithium batteries,
Styrofoam, wood, rubber, medical waste, large amounts of plastics,
and even entire trucks.

"AML is typically a young person's disease or a very old
person's disease," Burke said. "It's very rare that it strikes healthy
young men. We know that there are about 100 Iraq veterans who
were between the ages of 25 and 45, who came back from Iraq and
were diagnosed with AML. And all of them are gone. ...

"When we talked to the epidemiologists, they were just
stunned by the numbers they were seeing."

The plaintiffs include: Robyn Sachs, of Buffalo, NY,
whose husband Christopher J. Sachs, died in November 2008 of
complications from leukemia allegedly caused by his prolonged
exposure to KBR burn pit smoke, fumes and ash during his military
service in Iraq, [and many other GIs].

Source: *Corporate Crime Reporter*, May 4, 2009

Atlantic States Cast Iron Pipe Co., a Phillipsburg, New Jersey-
based division of McWane Inc. of Alabama, was sentenced last
week to pay a fine of $8 million for violations of environmental and

worker safety laws as well as obstructing the federal investigation of its conduct.

[The sentencing included four years of probation, during which the company will be subject to oversight by a court-appointed monitor].

The sentencing of the company followed sentencings last week of four former Atlantic States managers to federal prison terms.

"These sentences mete out just punishment for the company and its employees' disregard of the law which was demonstrated during the longest environmental crimes trial in this country's history for multiple violations of worker safety and environmental protection laws," said Associate Attorney General Thomas Perrelli.

The jury verdicts affirmed the government's charges that Atlantic States and the managers regularly discharged oil and other pollutants into the Delaware River, willfully polluted the air, and rigged emissions tests, concealed serious worker injuries from health and safety inspectors, and maintained a dangerous workplace that contributed to multiple injuries, including severe burns, broken bones and amputations and the death of one employee at the Phillipsburg plants.

The convictions represented the fifth time in two years that a McWane division either pled guilty or was convicted in federal court of environmental and worker safety crimes and obstruction.

The privately held McWane Inc. and its divisions are among the largest manufacturers in the world of ductile iron pipe, with more than a dozen plants in the United States and Canada.

Source: *Corporate Crime Reporter*, May 4, 2009

Comment: The *New York Times* published a series of investigative articles on McWane Inc. hazardous practices on January 8, 9, and 10, 2003, which won a Pulitzer Prize in 2004.

* * *

The Food and Drug Administration (FDA) should immediately increase its warning about the use of lubiprostone—available as Amitiza—because of serious adverse reaction, including the risk of abortion or premature labor if given to pregnant women, Public Citizen said in a petition filed last week with the agency.

"The FDA and drug makers should take every step possible to warn pregnant women and their doctors about the dangers of taking lubiprostone. The current label is grossly inadequate as it lacks useful information pertaining to the risks of drug-induced abortion in pregnant women who take this drug," said Sidney Wolfe, M.D., director of the Health Research Group at Public Citizen and its acting president. "There are safer, equally effective, alternative medications for pregnant women."

Source: *Corporate Crime Reporter*, May 11, 2009

Wal-Mart Fined $7,000 for Worker Death. The Occupational Safety and Health Administration (OSHA) has cited Wal-Mart Stores Inc. for inadequate crowd management following the November 28, 2008 death of an employee at its Valley Stream, N.Y. store.

The worker died of asphyxiation after he was knocked to the ground and trampled by a crowd of about 2,000 shoppers who surged into the store for its annual "Blitz Friday" pre-holiday sales event.

OSHA's inspection found that the store's employees were exposed to being crushed by the crowd due to the store's failures to implement reasonable and effective crowd management principles.

This failure includes providing employees with the necessary training and tools to safely manage the large crowd of shoppers. ...

The citation carries a proposed fine of $7,000, the maximum penalty amount for a serious violation allowed under the law.

Source: *Corporate Crime Reporter*, June 1, 2009

Comment: Seven thousand dollar fine, for avoidable negligence causing a worker's death is less than one hour's compensation for the CEO of Wal-Mart, who earns about $11,000 an hour, eight hours a day. Wal-Mart is still contesting this fine, having spent well over $2 million in legal fees.

* * *

"The top subprime lenders whose loans are largely blamed for triggering the global economic meltdown were owned or backed by giant banks now collecting billions of dollars in bailout money—including several that have paid huge fines to settle predatory lending charges.

"The banks that funded the subprime industry were not victims of an unforeseen financial collapse, as they have sometimes portrayed themselves, but enablers that bankrolled the type of lending threatening the financial system."

These, the writer of this piece goes on, are among the findings of the Center for Public Integrity's analysis of the data on the nearly 7.2 million subprime loans made from 2005 to 2007 in the run-up to the financial collapse.

Making hay while the sun shone, top-flight U.S. and European banks invested heavily in the subprime market. Among the investors were such "household names" as Lehman Brothers, Merrill Lynch, Citigroup, Credit Suisse First Boston and Goldman Sachs & Co. As the report shows, all of them were raking in profits and their executives were receiving a bounty of mega-bonuses "until the bottom fell out of the real estate market."

Source: *Corporate Crime Reporter*, June 15, 2009

Despite the Pentagon's hefty budget, Department of Defense personnel routinely accept free flights, accommodations, and hospitality from private and foreign interests which do business with the Pentagon, according to a Center for Public Integrity analysis of thousands of travel disclosure records.

The Center found that from 1998 through 2007, outside resources paid for more than 22,000 trips worth at least $26 million.

The travel was sponsored by an array of companies, foreign governments, and other groups.

These free trips have become riddled with conflicts of interest and are in need of stronger oversight and stiffer regulations, say watchdog groups.

"This is the kind of behavior that should be barred without a loophole," says Winslow Wheeler of the nonprofit Center for

Defense Information.
Source: *Corporate Crime Reporter*, June 15, 2009

Basel Action Network (BAN) has been at the forefront of exposing the "cyber-age" nightmare of electronic waste exportation to developing countries. In 2002 and 2005, BAN released two documentary films *Exporting Harm* and *The Digital Dump*, shining a spotlight on the horrors of the global e-waste trade and the very damaging impacts of toxic constituents in electronic products on the workers and environments of communities in Africa and China.

Recent studies in Guiyu, China, "ground zero" of the international waste trade, show some of the highest levels of dioxin, lead and other cancer-causing pollutants ever recorded. Blood levels in 80 percent of the children in Guiyu are elevated, and already demonstrable brain impairment has been recorded.

BAN estimates that 80 percent of the electronic waste given to recyclers in the U.S. and Canada does not get recycled in this continent, but is quickly exported due to a lack of adequate law, or inadequate enforcement of laws that do exist.

And BAN has created the e-Stewards Awards Initiative—a list of responsible e-cyclers that have agreed not to export hazardous e-wastes to developing countries.
Source: *Corporate Crime Reporter*, June 15, 2009

Friends of the Earth and Health Care Without Harm Europe released a report detailing the growing public health threat posed by nano-silver particles in consumer products.

"What we've learned is alarming," said Friends of the Earth's Ian Illuminato, one of the report's authors. "Major corporations are putting nano-silver into a wide variety of consumer products with virtually no oversight, and there are potentially serious health consequences as a result. The workers who manufacture these products, the families that use them, and the environment are all at risk."

Silver has long been known to be a potent antimicrobial agent. However, its use has exploded in recent years, in medical applications and also in many consumer products, including children's toys, babies' bottles, cosmetics, textiles, cleaning agents, chopping boards, refrigerators and dishwashers.

Much of the silver used in these products today is manufactured at the nano-scale, meaning it is present in extremely tiny particles that are especially potent. Studies suggest that the widespread use of nano-silver poses serious health and environmental risks and that it could promote anti-bacterial resistance, undermining its efficiency in a medical context.

"Inserting nano-silver into hundreds of new products could harm our bodies and the outdoor environments into which it's released," said Illuminato. "Nano-silver doesn't distinguish between good and bad bacteria—it kills all bacteria with which it interacts, many of which are necessary for our survival and the survival of other living organisms."

"Do we really need to coat cups, bowls and cutting boards, personal care products, children's toys and infant products in nano-silver for 'hygienic reasons?'" asked report coauthor Dr. Rye Senjen, Friends of the Earth Australia's nanotechnology expert. "Overuse of this extreme germ killer poses a serious public health risk."

"We are playing with fire, especially at a time when anti-bacterial resistance is an ever increasing medical problem globally," Dr. Senjen said.

The report also warns that nano-silver may leach out of products such as clothing, cosmetics, and washing machines and find its way into water systems and potentially interfere with the treatment of waste water and sewage.

Friends of the Earth is calling for an immediate moratorium on the commercial release of products that contain manufactured nano-silver until nanotechnology-specific regulation is put in place to protect the public, workers, and the environment, until all products containing nano-silver are labeled as such, and until the public is involved in decision making about the use of this particle.

Source: *Corporate Crime Reporter*, June 15, 2009

The European Commission fined E.ON AG and its subsidiary

E.ON Ruhrgas AG (of Germany) and GDF Suez SA (of France) $769 million each for agreeing in 1975, when they decided to jointly build the MEGAL pipeline across Germany, to import Russian gas into Germany and France, not to sell gas transported over this pipeline in each other's home markets. They maintained the market-sharing agreement after European gas markets were liberalized and only abandoned it definitely in 2005.

Source: *Corporate Crime Reporter*, July 13, 2009

Comment: It would be noteworthy to know how much more European consumers paid for their natural gas above and beyond the total of the fines to see how much profit these corporate antitrust crimes paid!

* * *

A major new study released last week by Americans for Insurance Reform finds that premiums and claims for doctors both have dropped significantly in recent years while the medical malpractice insurance industry is enjoying remarkable profits in light of the global economic collapse.

It concludes that further limiting the liability of negligent doctors and unsafe hospitals is not only unjustified, but also would have almost no impact on lowering this country's overall health care expenditures.

The report, titled *True Risk: Medical Liability, Malpractice Insurance and Health Care,* was written by G. Cassell-Stiga and Joanne Doroshow of the Center for Justice & Democracy, and actuary J. Robert Hunter of the Consumer Federation of America (CFA), former Commissioner of Insurance for Texas and former Federal Insurance Administrator under Presidents Ford and Carter.

"Thirty years of inflation-adjusted data show that medical malpractice premiums are the lowest they have been in this entire period," Hunter said. "This is in no small part due to the fact that claims have fallen like a rock, down 45 percent since 2000."

"The periodic premium spikes we see in the data are not related to claims but to the economic cycle of insurers and to drops in investment income. Since prices have not declined as much as claims have, medical malpractice insurer profits are higher than the rest of the property casualty industry, which has been remarkably profitable over the last five years.

"Our research makes clear that medical malpractice claims and premiums have almost no impact on the cost of health care. Medical malpractice premiums are less than one-half of one percent of overall health care costs, and medical malpractice claims are a mere one-fifth of one percent of health care costs."

Doroshow said that "insurers are raking in money and belittling the fact that hundreds of thousands of patients are killed or injured due to medical negligence each year."

Source: *Corporate Crime Reporter*, July 27, 2009

Comment: During the Congressional debate on health insurance reform, Republicans over and over again demanded further federal restrictions on the right of injured patients to sue reckless, incompetent physicians and negligent hospitals. They wildly exaggerated the costs and ignored the 100,000 malpractice-caused American deaths each year plus more injuries and sicknesses. Their callous comments ignored these enormous preventable causalities and attacked the trial lawyers for frivolous suits that they could never substantiate. Fortunately their crude cruelty got them nowhere. Over 90 percent of medical malpractice doesn't even result in a claim, so difficult and uphill are the obstacles for these innocent victims.

* * *

Reproductive health in the United States is declining as exposure to dangerous chemicals is rising, according to a data-rich slide show released by the Center for American Progress titled *Reproductive Roulette: Declining Reproductive Health, Dangerous Chemicals, and a New Way Forward*.

Fertility problems, miscarriages, preterm births, and birth defects are all up. Meanwhile, the number of chemicals registered for commercial use now stands at 30,000—a 30 percent increase since 1979.

These trends in reproductive health are not simply the result of women postponing motherhood. In fact, women under 25 and women between 25 and 34 report an increasing number of fertility problems. Men and boys are also experiencing problems. Average sperm count appears to be steadily declining, and there are rising rates of male genital birth defects such as hypospadias, a condition in which the urethra does not develop properly.

"Americans are regularly exposed to dangerous chemicals that we know can harm reproductive health. These exposures appear to be taking a disturbing toll," said Reece Rushing, author of the report.

Chemical exposures occur in a variety of ways, including through industrial releases, contaminated food, household products and cosmetics, and [in a] workplace where chemicals are used. Tests of blood and urine confirm rising and widespread exposure to a chemical soup of metals, pesticides, plasticizers, and other substances, many of which are dangerous to reproductive health. Young children are often exposed to significantly higher relative levels of these chemicals than adults. Racial and ethnic minorities are also exposed at higher levels.

Source: *Corporate Crime Reporter*, July 27, 2009

Comment: Silent, cumulative violence of these chemicals does not produce strong reactions as would an alley mugging or a Peeping Tom. That is why prevention—foreseeing and forestalling—is so important. This is the precautionary principle which puts the burden of proving that chemicals are safe onto the producers and vendors, not on the unequipped, un-sensing victims.

* * *

Thirty-two people—doctors and health care executives—were indicted last week for schemes to submit more than $16 million in false Medicare claims … [their apprehension being part of the] continuing operation of the Medicare Fraud Strike Force in Houston. The indictments were for defrauding the Medicare program, and criminal false claims.

The Strike Force operations in Houston have identified the primary fraud schemes as those related to false billing for "arthritis kits," power wheelchairs and enteral feeding supplies. The indictments charged that beneficiaries were deceased at the time they allegedly received the items.

Source: *Corporate Crime Reporter*, August 3, 2009

Comment: Tens of billions of dollars are defrauded from Medicare, yet the Congress declines to beef up the investigative and prosecutorial resources of the government.

* * *

"Medicare frauds are often inelegant, but they're outrageously lucrative and relatively low-risk. So lucrative, and so low-risk, the FBI reports, that a number of cocaine dealers in Florida and California have switched from illicit drugs to Medicare fraud.

"Medicare loses billions of dollars to fraud each year. 'Those billions of dollars,' said Eric Holder, U.S. attorney general, 'represent health care dollars' that could be spent on medicine or care or hospital visits, 'but instead are wasted on greed.'"

Jay Weaver, writing for the *AARP Bulletin*, adds that while Medicare is attempting to fight against this crime wave, Congress has refused to provide needed funds. As far back as 2005, Congress denied Medicare's request for funds for policing these frauds. This denial is a piece of fiscal foolishness in that "the agency's Office of Inspector General says that every dollar spent protecting the program returns $17."

Source: "Criminals Bilk Medicare of Billions Each Year," *AARP Bulletin*, November 1, 2009 (by Jay Weaver)

The Justice Department last week filed a False Claims Act lawsuit against First Choice Armor & Equipment Inc. and its founder Edward Dovner for submitting false claims for bullet-proof vests purchased by the United States for federal, state, local and tribal and law enforcement agencies.

First Choice, which manufactured and sold bullet-proof vests containing Zylon fiber from 2000-2005, marketed its vests to law enforcement agencies as a thinner and more lightweight alternative to other bullet-proof vests.

Federal officials alleged that at the same time First Choice was selling its Zylon bulletproof vests, the company and its founder knew of significant manufacturing and degradation problems in the Zylon fiber that rendered the material unsafe for ballistic protection.

In fact, when the Justice Department's National Institute of Justice tested eight of First Choice's bullet-proof vests in 2005, all failed.

The government alleges that after learning of the investigation into Zylon bullet-proof vests, defendants removed more than $5 million from First Choice. Mr. Dovner then purchased a Ferrari, a Maserati, and a private jet through various shell companies.

"By providing defective bullet-proof vests to the nation's law enforcement officers, First Choice put the lives of those officers at risk," stated Tony West, Assistant Attorney General for the Civil Division of the Department of Justice. ...

The government has previously settled for more than $47 million with five other entities that allegedly were involved in the manufacture or sale of defective Zylon vests.

Source: *Corporate Crime Reporter*, August 10, 2009

More than one of every five requests for medical claims for insured patients, even when recommended by a patient's physician, are rejected by California's largest private insurers, amounting to very real death panels in practice daily in the nation's biggest state, according to data released last week by the California Nurses Association.

From 2002 through June 30, 2009, the six largest insurers operating in California rejected 31.2 million claims for care—21 percent of all claims. ...

"The reality for patients today is a daily, cold-hearted rejection of the desperately needed medical care by the nation's biggest and wealthiest insurance companies simply because they don't want to pay for it," said Deborah Burger, RN, CAN/NNOC [National Nurses Organizing Committee] co-president.

Rejection rates are escalating. PacifiCare denied 40 percent of all California claims in the first six months of 2009. Cigna, which gained notoriety two years ago for denying a liver transplant to 17-year-old Nataline Sarkisyan of Northridge, California, and then reversing itself, tragically too late to save her life, was still rejecting one-third of all claims for the first half of 2009.

California Blues rejected 28 percent of claims in the first half of 2009.

Kaiser Permanente, which denied 28 percent of all claims in the first half of 2009, was one of two systems to reject options for radiation and chemotherapy for 57year-old Bob Scott of Sacramento after his diagnosis of a brain tumor in 2005.

"The reason cited was his age," says wife Cheryl Scott, RN. "He had been in perfect health all his life. This was his first problem other than a sprained ankle. He died six months later."

Rejection of care is a very lucrative business for the insurance giants. The top 18 insurance giants racked up $15.9 billion in profits last year.

"Nothing in any of the major bills advancing in the Senate or House or proposed by the [Obama] administration would challenge this [denial of care] practice," said Burger. "The United State remains the only country in the industrialized world where human lives are sacrificed for private profit, a national disgrace that seems on the verge of perpetuation," she said.

Source: *Corporate Crime Reporter*, September 7, 2009

Comment: Now you see how accurate was *Business Week's* cover story of August 17, 2009, that said "The Health Insurers Have Already Won" in Congress. The Pay or Die health insurance cabal continues in the Land of the Free, Home of the Brave. A 2010 fact sheet titled: Insurance Companies Prosper, Families Suffer: Our Broken Health Insurance System notes: "Last year, as working families struggled with rising health care costs and a recession, the five largest health insurance companies—WellPoint, UnitedHealth

Group, Cigna, Aetna, and Humana—took in combined profits of $12.2 billion, up 56 percent over 2008."

* * *

Malcolm Sparrow, an applied mathematician, is a professor of public management at Harvard's Kennedy School. He believes the percentage of health care fraud could be as high as 20 percent or even 30 percent of all health care expenditures. In the range of $400 [billion] to $600 billion is being lost each year. Sparrow told the *Corporate Crime Reporter*, "We don't know" with any exactitude. "We should know. The government knows how to measure it, but is avoiding doing it. The news would be too bad."

"The method behind any measurement is this—you pick a random sample of claims. You review them seriously to find out if you should have paid them," Sparrow said.

"While the government isn't controlling health care fraud aimed at public expenditures, the private health insurance industry isn't doing a better job of it," Sparrow says.

Across the board, both public and private programs are spending only about one tenth of one percent on fraud control programs. To bring the problem under control, Sparrow suggests an expenditure of about one percent.

"But that's ten times the current level of investment," says Sparrow. "So, we should actually increase the level of attention, dedication and resources by a factor of ten or more. Politically, that is simply not going to happen. Certainly, not while there is uncertainty about whether this is a significant problem or not.

"Which is why I get back to rule number one—measure the problem, put the facts on the table, so that everybody can see how much we are losing.

"I actually have in front of me a stack of reports from the last eight years. Dead patients showing up in Medicare and Medicaid claims all around the country. Deported patients that have been previously banished from the country, according to INS. Banished from the country, and not allowed back in. But they still get Medicare.

"Incarcerated patients. Folks in prison who are supposed to be covered by different health insurance. The final insult, revealed last year by the Senate Permanent Committee on Investigations—dead doctors showing up as prescribing or referring physicians. In many cases, doctors who had been dead more than ten years when they ordered equipment or drugs or made a referral."

Source: *Corporate Crime Reporter*, September 14, 2009

Comment: Sparrow's best estimate, lacking this comprehensive sampling he described, is between $250 billion and $500 billion. He says: "When you talk to investigators on the street and people who actually investigate in high fraud areas, the idea that we are losing 20 or 24 percent is not at all implausible. Can I prove that is how much we are losing? No. You would actually have to run a measurement program correctly."

* * *

Almost four decades ago, Congress passed the Clean Water Act to force polluters to disclose the toxins they dump into waterways and to give regulators the power to fine or jail offenders.

But in recent years, violations of the Clean Water Act have risen steadily across the nation, an extensive review of water pollution records by *The New York Times* found.

In the last five years alone, chemical factories, manufacturing plants and other workplaces have violated water pollution laws more than half a million times.

The violations range from failing to report emissions to dumping toxins at concentrations regulators say might contribute to cancer, birth defects and other illnesses.

However, the vast majority of those polluters have escaped punishment.

The *Times* obtained hundreds of thousands of water pollution records through Freedom of Information Act requests to every state and the EPA, and compiled a national database of water pollution violations that is more comprehensive than those maintained by states or the EPA.

In addition, the *Times* interviewed more than 250 state and federal regulators, water-system managers, environmental advocates and scientists.

That research shows that an estimated one in 10 Americans have been exposed to drinking water that contains dangerous chemicals or fails to meet a federal health benchmark in other ways.

Because most of today's water pollution has no scent or taste, many people who consume dangerous chemicals do not realize it, even after they become sick, researchers say.

But an estimated 19.5 million Americans fall ill each year from drinking water contaminated with parasites, bacteria or viruses, according to a study published last year in the scientific journal *Reviews of Environmental Contamination and Toxicology*. That figure does not include illnesses caused by other chemicals and toxins.

Source: *Corporate Crime Reporter*, September 23, 2009

"Hundreds of cases have been brought against big corporations over the years alleging they ripped off the federal government and violated the False Claims Act.

"The government has recovered hundreds of millions of dollars in settlement of those cases.

"But few individual executives of those corporations have been criminally prosecuted and sent to jail."

So begins this significant article about how members of corporate management, no matter how dirty their hands, never seem to receive criminal case penalties. In fact, in the 100 biggest False Claims Act cases, there was not a single one in which an executive was brought up on criminal charges.

Contrast that, the writer says, to what would happen to an individual who was not acting as part of a corporation and stole from the federal government. Could this individual so easily escape hard time and even continue to receive later government contracts?

Patrick Burns of Taxpayers Against Fraud points to the double standard by which, if "you are an individual and you steal $140,000 from the government," jail is your next stop. "But if you are a big corporation ... and you grab $140 million, you pay a fine." None of the company's top execs see the inside of the cell, and, as often as not, next year the firm gets another government contract.

Source: *Corporate Crime Reporter*, September 28, 2009

The latest available data from the Justice Department show that during January 2009 the government reported 129 new government regulatory prosecutions.

According to the case-by-case information analyzed by the Transactional Records Access Clearinghouse (TRAC), this number is down 28.3 percent over the previous month.

When monthly 2009 prosecutions of this type are compared with those of the same period in the previous year, the number of filings was down 18.6 percent.

Prosecutions over the past year are still much lower than they were five years ago.

Overall, the data show that prosecutions of this type are down 16.2 percent from levels reported in 2004.

Source: *Corporate Crime Reporter*, May 4, 2009

Comment: These declines in regulatory prosecutions are occurring in the midst of a corporate crime wave and grossly inadequate regulatory agency budgets whose fines could be revenues far in excess of the agencies' enforcement costs.

* * *

More than 500 hard-core international cartels have been busted since 1990. That's the key finding of a paper released last week by the American Antitrust Institute.

The paper was written by John Conner, a professor of agricultural economics at Purdue University.

The paper found 516 private hard-core cartels that were subject to government or private legal actions—formal investigation, damages suits, fine, or consent decrees—between January 1990 and December 2008.

Each cartel had participants with headquarters in two or more nations. The cartels involved more than 6,000 companies. About 2,400 parent companies were fined. At least 373 individual, named executives have been penalized, hundreds more were guilty but immunized, and thousands more guilty but not prosecuted, Connor found.

Most cartels sell industrialized goods. Fourteen cartels sold agricultural or mining raw materials, 208 intermediate industrial materials, 23 industrialized capital goods, 34 undifferentiated consumer materials, 40 differentiated consumer goods and 166 business or consumer services.

Connor said that international cartels are being assaulted worldwide on all fronts.

Source: *Corporate Crime Reporter*, October 12, 2009

Comment: Cartels are formed to fix prices, allocate markets, exclude competitors and engage in other activities that are criminal violations in most countries. The notorious international vitamins cartel, broken up by the U.S. government a few years ago, stole many billions of dollars from consumers who were forced to pay higher prices.

* * *

Banks and credit unions collected nearly $24 billion in overdraft fees last year, an increase of 35 percent from just two years earlier, a new study by the Center for Responsible Lending (CRL) shows.

The explosion in overdraft charges has drained the wallet of as many as 51 million Americans whose accounts become overdrawn annually.

It is particularly harmful to financially vulnerable families already hit hard by the recession.

"Banks and credit unions have become so sophisticated in driving up overdrafts that Americans now pay more in overdraft fees every year than they do for books, cereal, or fresh vegetables," said CRL senior researcher Leslie Parrish.

The most common trigger of overdraft fees are small debit

card transactions that could easily be denied for no fee.

card transactions that could easily be denied for no fee.

This is how things used to work, and according to a 2008 nationally representative survey, it's what the large majority of people prefer.

Thousands of bank and credit union customers have complained to federal regulators that overdraft policies are unfair.

Customers typically haven't explicitly agreed to these high-cost overdraft loan programs but are automatically enrolled by their bank.

When consumers try to avoid these abusive fees, they often find themselves tripped up when, for example, institutions needlessly delay posting deposits or when they process purchases from largest to smallest to purposely generate multiple overdrafts.

And because overdrawing an account by just a few dollars triggers a fee averaging $34, cash-stripped households often are thrust even further into debt by this overdraft "protection."

The report recommended that policymakers: "Require that institutions deny debit card purchases and ATM withdrawals, without charge, if the funds aren't there; [and] require that overdraft fees bear some relationship to a lender's cost of covering a shortfall."

Source: *Corporate Crime Reporter*, October 12, 2009

Comment: Some years ago, the Federal Reserve estimated the cost of a bounced check to be $1.50 to the bank, including the cost of fraud losses. Some profit center, aye?

* * *

The Government Accountability Office (GAO), an investigative oversight arm of Congress, released a report [showing] that while importers report information about food shipments to the Customs agency, that agency's computer system does not notify the Food and Drug Administration (FDA) or the U.S. Department of Agriculture's Food Safety and Inspection Service when shipments arrive at the border, increasing the risk that contaminated food passes through border checkpoints undetected.

The report found that Customs and FDA do not use a unique identification number for importers, making it difficult for FDA to track high-risk imports and importers.

The report also found that FDA lacks the authority to fine importers who don't comply with its regulations. As a result, importers can ignore rules against selling food shipments before they are cleared by FDA.

Source: *Corporate Crime Reporter*, October 19, 2009

Comment: Astonishingly, the U.S. imports about three quarters as much food by dollar value as it exports. Increasingly, contaminated imported food, scarcely inspected by Customs (1 percent inspected), is reaching and sickening consumers. From China has come polluted fish, raised on fish farms, and other contaminated food products.

* * *

The new chairman of the Consumer Product Safety Commission (CPSC) said she would ask China to help pay for the billions of dollars in damage to U.S. homes blamed on Chinese-made drywall, the *Wall Street Journal* reported last week.

`"I will find out if any discussions are going on in China about the costs, are they prepared to participate in providing funds, and what would it take for that to occur," CPSC Chairman Inez Tenenbaum said in an interview ahead of a trip to China next week for a biennial U.S.-China consumer product safety summit.

Ms. Tenenbaum said she also planned to start discussion with Chinese officials on whether the U.S. needs a regulatory standard for drywall composition. "I think we need one," she said.

The CPSC has received about 1,500 reports from residents in 27 states, the District of Columbia and Puerto Rico, who blame health problems and property damage on Chinese drywall in their homes. State and local authorities have received similar reports that include homeowner complaints about respiratory problems, bloody noses and recurrent headaches, the *Journal* reported.

The Chinese drywall, also known as gypsum or wallboard, is

under investigation for emitting sulfide fumes suspected of causing the homeowner complaints. As many as 100,000 homes across the country have the suspect drywall, most of them built in 2006 and 2007.

Source: *Corporate Crime Reporter*, October 19, 2009

California AG Brown Sues State Street Bank for Massive Fraud Against CalPERS. Seeking to recover more than $200 million in illegal overcharges and penalties, California Attorney General Edmund G. Brown Jr. last week sued State Street Bank and Trust—one of the world's leading providers of financial services to institutional investors—for committing "unconscionable fraud" against California's two largest pension funds, CalPERS and CalSTRS.

The lawsuit contends that Boston-based State Street illegally over-charged CalPERS and CalSTRS for the costs of executing foreign currency trades since 2001.

"Over a period of eight years, State Street bankers committed unconscionable fraud by misappropriating millions of dollars that rightfully belonged to California's public pension funds," Brown said. "This is just the latest example of how clever financial traders violate laws and rip off the public trust."

The case was originally filed under seal by whistleblowers [who called themselves]—"Associates Against FX Insider Trading," who alleged that State Street added a secret and substantial markup to the price of interbank foreign currency.

Subsequently Brown's investigation revealed that State Street was indeed overcharging the two funds. Despite being contractually obligated to charge the interbank rate at the precise time of the trade, State Street consistently charged at or near the highest rate of the day, even if the interbank rate was lower at the time of the trade.

State Street concealed the fraud by deliberately failing to include time stamp data in its reports, so that the pension fund could not determine the true execution costs by verifying when State Street actually executed the trades, Brown asserted.

Commenting on this deception, one State Street senior vice president said to another executive that "... if providing execution costs will give [CalPERS] any insight into how much we make off of FX transactions, I will be shocked if [State Street] or anyone would agree to reveal the information."
Source: *Corporate Crime Reporter*, October, 26 2009

Comment: Readers may wonder if State Street did this to other pension funds in other states and, if so, whether the attorneys general in those cases moved to recover the overcharges plus penalties and costs. It seems not, to our knowledge, and leaves one to wonder how much this sprawling crime has paid State Street, minus what they may have to reimburse the California pension funds.

* * *

Mylan Pharmaceuticals, UDL Laboratories, AstraZeneca Pharmaceuticals and Ortho McNeil Pharmaceuticals have entered into settlement agreements for a total of $124 million to resolve claims that they violated the False Claims Act by failing to pay appropriate rebates to state Medicaid programs for drugs paid for by those programs.
Source: *Corporate Crime Reporter*, October 26, 2009

The nation's largest nursing home pharmacy, Omnicare Inc. of Covington, Kentucky, will pay $98 million, and drug manufacturer, WAX Pharmaceuticals of Weston, Florida, will pay $14 million to resolve allegations that Omnicare engaged in kickback schemes with several parties, including WAX.
Approximately $68.5 million of the settlement proceeds will go to the United States, while $43.5 million has been allocated to cover Medicaid program claims by participating states.
Source: *Corporate Crime Reporter*, November 9, 2009

Most Food Ads on Nickelodeon are for Junk Food. Nearly 80 percent of food ads on the popular children's network Nickelodeon are for foods of poor nutritional quality, according to an analysis conducted by the Center for Science in the Public Interest (CSPI).

That represents a modest and not quite statistically significant drop from 2005, when CSPO researchers found that about 90 percent of food ads on Nick were for junk food.

Between the 2005 and 2009 studies, the food industry instituted a self-regulatory program through the Council of Better Business Bureaus: the Children's Food and Beverage Advertising Initiative (CFBAI).

CSPI also examined the practices of the food companies that participate in that self-regulatory program.

Of the 452 foods and beverages that companies say are acceptable to market to children, CSPI found that 267, or nearly 60 percent, do not meet CSPI's recommended nutrition standards for food marketing to children, such as General Mills' Cookie Crisp and Reese's Puffs cereals, Kellogg's Apple Jacks and Cocoa Krispies cereals, Kellogg's Rice Krispies Treats, Campbell's Goldfish crackers and SpaghettiOs, Kraft's Macaroni & Cheese, and many Unilever Popsicles.

"While industry self-regulation is providing some useful benchmarks, it's clearly not shielding children from junk food advertising, on Nick and elsewhere," said CSPI nutrition policy director Margo G. Wootan, "It's a modest start, but not sufficient to arrest children's poor eating habits and the sky-high rates of childhood obesity."

"None of the 10 products PepsiCo says are appropriate to market to children actually are according to CPSI's standards.

Only three of 47 Kraft-approved products, one of eight McDonald's-approved meals and 22 of 86 General Mills-approved products met CSPI's standards. ...

"Nickelodeon should be ashamed that it earns so much money from carrying commercials that promote obesity, diabetes, and other health problems in young children," Wootan said. "If media and food companies don't do a better job exercising corporate responsibility when they market foods to children, Congress and the FTC will need to step in to protect kids' health."

Source: *Corporate Crime Reporter*, November 30, 2009

Comment: Corporate marketing directly to children, undermining parental authority and selling harmful foods constitute electronic child molestation and are deceptive practices that the FTC could prohibit. More FTC authority by Congress to protect these children would be helpful also.

* * *

A new report from China Labor Watch's (CLW) documented substandard working and living conditions for Chinese workers toiling to make products for Wal-Mart.

According to China Labor Watch, roughly 1,800 workers at the Dashing Decoration Company in Dongguan City specialize in producing candles and Christmas lights for Wal-Mart.

The CLW reports document that Dashing workers:

- Fail to receive basic information required by the Labor Contract Law.
- Sometimes work 24 consecutive hours and only get two days off per month.
- Work mandatory overtime hours without receiving the legal overtime compensation. Workers who refuse will receive a penalty equivalent to three days wages.
- Are asked to lie during audits and sign false pay stubs to deceive clients.
- Live in employer-provided housing with inhuman conditions. Bathrooms have no running water, canteen sanitation is poor and fees are deducted from wages regardless of whether workers can eat there.
- Pay nine days wages in fines for absence of more than half a day and lose wages if production quotas are not met.
- The majority of products sold in Wal-Mart's shelves are manufactured overseas, and China is home to thousands of factories supplying the giant retailer.

Source: *Corporate Crime Reporter*, December 7, 2009

Comment: While Wal-Mart retains its U.S. headquarters in Bentonville, Arkansas, its world headquarters are now in China, so the company knows what is going on.

* * *

WALL STREET FIRMS—TOO BIG TO PUNISH. Forget too big to fail. In the eyes of federal regulators, many Wall Street firms are too big to punish.

During the past three years, some of the nation's largest financial firms have been accused by the government of cheating or misleading clients and ripping off tens of thousands of consumers of their investments.

But despite these findings, these financial giants got, sometimes repeatedly, special exemptions from the Securities and Exchange Commission (SEC) that have saved them from a regulatory death penalty that could have decimated their lucrative mutual funds businesses.

That's according to a report from McClatchy News Service last week.

Among the more than a dozen firms that have gotten these SEC get-out-of-jail cards (known as section 9(c) waivers) since January 2007 are some of Wall Street's biggest, including Bank of America, Citigroup and American International Group (AIG).

In fact, the last time the SEC's staff could recall a waiver being turned down was in 1978, McClatchy News reported. ...

"The SEC has a miserable record of policing and keeping track of recidivism even of prior violations," said James Cox, a Duke University Law professor and an expert on financial regulations. "I think it's not uncommon and I think it's a problem."

Source: *Corporate Crime Reporter*, December 14, 2009

How do financial crooks escape the law? The Securities and Exchange Commission and the Commodity Futures Trading Commission (CFTC) can't bring ... criminal charges themselves [against fraud]. ... Hundreds of people get away without jail time. Nearly two-thirds of all CFTC cases referred to the

Justice Department for criminal prosecution are rejected. Justice lawyers are overworked, and many lack the training to prosecute complicated securities or commodity futures cases. Giving the CFTC and the SEC criminal authority would make more efficient and effective use of government resources and could deter those thinking of committing a financial crime.

Source: Bart Chilton, a member of the CFTC

"Nearly one year after the collapse of Lehman Brothers sent shock waves across the globe, the world is a different place," according to David Enrich, writing in the *Wall Street Journal*. "The investment bank's messy death," he goes on, had major repercussions, pushing America deeper into a major recession, causing the federal government to step in and regulate financial markets, and bringing the public notice that these markets did not seem to be able to function without some government direction.

Yet even with these sea changes in the way things work, many aspects of our financial sector seem untouched by the catastrophe, Enrich notes. The banks are unchastened, again handing out hefty bonuses and compensations. At the same time, the "exotic financial products," nearly the same ones that brought down the economy when they proved unreliable, are again on sale. It seems that not only are banks back in that game, but their "appetite for risk has grown."

Source: *Wall Street Journal*, September 9, 2009 (by David Enrich)

"Susan Halley didn't have the money. The lawyer trying to collect it was sure she could find some. 'You have a car, right?' the lawyer said, as Ms. Halley recalled. 'That's a luxury.' The car, an $11,000 Mitsubishi bought with a loan, was how she got to work. Ms. Halley was lost in the land of medical debt, a place where mind-boggling bills rain down like meteorites, crushing the solvent, the prudent, the responsible."

So begins a biting piece by Jim Dwyer of the *New York Times*, in which his research uncovered that "a study of 2007 bankruptcy filings found that nearly two-thirds were caused by medical bills."

To give a little more background on how Halley ended up in this no-win situation, Dwyer explains, "On the Saturday of Memorial Day weekend five years ago, Ms. Halley had her favorite meal, the cheeseburger deluxe, at a diner near her home in Queens. She was 25 years old and lived with her mother. She had graduated from Baruch College in Manhattan and was getting a master's degree in special education at Touro College. She also had a job: a little more than two months earlier, she had gone to work for a nonprofit group that helped disabled people."

The next evening she began suffering intestinal pain and sought help from her family doctor, but, when this didn't end the discomfort, she checked into the emergency room at the North Shore University Hospital/Manhasset.

She knew this would hurt her financially because she hadn't been at her new job long enough to receive insurance coverage, so she would have to pay everything out of pocket. When she was admitted, it was found out that she was bleeding internally, and though the cause was never learned, she had a six-day hospital stay.

The medical billing department hardly gave her time to rest before they started looking to collect for her visit. As Halley recalls, "I got out of the hospital after six days on Monday. They called me on a Saturday, at home, requesting that I pay this bill. They wanted $400 a month."

Adding together her $27,000 hospital tab and that for doctors' visits, she was out $29,000. That was nearly her whole yearly income, which was, pretax, $33,000.

She tried to bargain the bill collector down, saying she could pay $200 a month, but he wouldn't budge, she says, adding, "They sent me the itemized bill, and most of it you can't understand, because it's all code."

Source: *New York Times*, September 13, 2009 (by Jim Dwyer)

"Jennifer Hall-Massey knows not to drink the tap water in her home near Charleston, WV.

"In fact, her entire family tries to avoid any contact with the water.

"Her youngest son has scabs on his arms, legs and chest where the bathwater polluted with lead, nickel and other heavy metals caused painful rashes. Many of his brother's teeth were capped to replace enamel that was eaten away."

Such physical problems stemming from water usage are hardly confined to this one family, but, the author of this *Times* article explains, are spread throughout the neighborhood. And a scientific evaluation revealed the source of the problem: the tap water was laced with arsenic, barium, lead, manganese and other chemicals in such high amounts that federal regulators say its usage could damage the nervous system and kidneys as well as possibly lead to cancer.

Equally shocking, this community is not some isolated backwater in the Appalachian Mountains but in a town 17 miles from the state capital. And Mrs. Hall-Massey is not a poor dirt farmer, but a senior accountant in one of the largest banks in the state. She, herself, can hardly believe the situation, questioning, "How can we get digital cable and Internet in our homes, but not clean water?"

Mrs. Hall-Massey and 264 neighbors decided to get together and sue nine local coal companies, who they suspected of polluting the water. When their lawyer looked into the case, he found that these companies, who legally had to tell the government what pollutants they were discarding, "had disclosed in reports to regulators that they were pumping into the ground illegal concentrations of chemicals—the same pollutants that flowed from residents' taps."

Yet the state regulators had never exacted any punishment from these corporate law breakers. Moreover, unfortunately, the West Virginian regulators are hardly exceptionally lax. As the author underlines, in this and other states, "in the last five years alone, chemical factories, manufacturing plants and other workplaces have violated water pollution laws more than half a million times," and, in the majority of cases, gotten off scot free.

The state agencies have turned a blind eye to the deeds of these miscreants while the EPA, which should be taking up the slack when state regulators fall down on the job, has been equally dilatory.

The West Virginia problem has been brewing a long time, according to the *Times* account. For many years, the area around the troubled community was coal-mining territory, but the well water was clean and unpolluted, at least until about 10 years ago when things went bad. "Awful smells began coming from local taps," the water was discolored and oily, and rusty rings appeared in tubs and washing machines. It seems no coincidence that this turn for the worse occurred at about the time coal companies began "pumping industrial waste into the ground."

Records revealed the coal companies began pouring coal slurry and sludge into lagoons or injecting it directly into the earth, disposing of more than 1.9 billion gallons through the latter practice by 2004.

"Sometimes," the *Times* reports, "these concentrations exceeded legal limits by as much as 1,000 percent." The chemicals being so casually put into the environment were those that are known to "contribute to cancer, organ failures and other diseases."

Not only did the West Virginia state regulators not fine or otherwise penalize these firms, they did not even tell these law-breaking companies that the government was aware of their misdeeds.

Source: *New York Times*, September 3, 2009 (by Charles Duhigg)

* * *

When you heat up water, the second stage is transition boiling. This occurs as the water gets hotter throughout and bubbles emerge from deep in the liquid. Now that you've heard of such corporate abuses as the global dumping of e-waste, water pollution and the scandal of overdraft fees, I reckon you may be at this second stage. Now the bubbles of rage are emerging not just intellectually, from your head, but from deep within, emotionally from your heart.

* * *

"When Dan Gerkey was trying to get into better shape a few years ago, he tried out a dietary supplement from a local store that promised to help build his strength. At first, the stuff worked. But after several weeks the police officer, who lives in Fraser, Michigan, started feeling exhausted, and his wife noticed a yellowish tinge in his eyes."

As this eye-opening *Wall Street Journal* piece by Anna Wilde Matthews tells the tale, Gerkey's skin began itching and yellowing. It took some time but eventually a liver specialist at Henry Ford Health System in Detroit traced his problems to a steroid in the supplement, one which was proving harmful to his liver.

Clearly, dietary supplements are not always trustworthy, and Gerkey's case, though exceptional, is far from unprecedented. In 2004, Ephedra, a herbal concoction recommended for weight loss, had to be withdrawn from sale upon the finding that it could contribute to strokes and heart disease.

It turns out, according to new findings from the FDA, that some of these "herbal" supplements are not what they are promoted to be, that is, natural. Instead, they may contain, among unlisted ingredients, performance-boosting drugs and pharmaceuticals.

And the alarm such recent revelations is causing is understandable in that, as figures released by the Council for Responsible Nutrition (an industry trade group) show, a full two-thirds of Americans take some type of natural supplement, whether in the form of vitamins, minerals or other herbal products.

Government regulation of these supplements is hardly overly strict. New products, being reviewed by the FDA, can be sold while they are still being studied, and older products, ones that were sold prior to 1994, don't face any form of retroactive review whatsoever. This is why consumer advocates think the FDA should have more stringent regulations on what it lets into the marketplace.

Source: *Wall Street Journal*, September 8, 2009 (by Anna Wilde Matthews)

"After the mortgage business imploded last year, Wall Street investment banks began searching for another big idea to make money....

"The bankers plan to buy 'life settlements,' life insurance policies that ill and elderly people sell for cash, $400,000 for a $1 million policy, say, depending on the life expectancy of the insured person. Then they plan to 'securitize' these policies, in Wall Street jargon, by packaging hundreds or thousands together into bonds. They will then resell those bonds to investors like big pension funds, who will receive the payouts when people with the insurance die."

This macabre turn of events, as discussed in this *New York Times* piece, involves an element of gambling in that the sooner the seller drops dead, the larger the return for the investor. Of course, if the seller turns out to be long-lived, the purchaser would lose out. The big winner, though, is Wall Street, where firms make a handsome fee from creating, merchandising and trading the securities.

Goldman Sachs is pioneering in the field, having created "a tradable index of life settlements" as well as having set up an in-house group to sell life settlements.

The whole situation smacks of the recent heyday, preceding the financial collapse, when companies like Goldman Sachs came up with new-fangled, risky, but lucrative-in-the-short-term financial instruments, such as "credit-default swaps, structured investment vehicles, collateralized debt obligations." These investments made money fast, but are now seen as big contributors, along with the subprime mortgages, to our economy's disastrous economic dip.

This new investment suggests Wall Street is cooking up new dangers for the economy. If these settlements take off in the marketplace, it means seniors may be targets. Last April, Stephen Leimberg, who has written on life settlements, spoke of these dangers to a Senate Special Committee on Aging. He warned, "Predators in the life settlement market have the motive, means and, if left unchecked by legislators and regulators and by their own community, the opportunity to take advantage of seniors."

Source: *New York Times*, September 6, 2009

Comment: There they go again. As Stephen Weisbart, senior vice president and chief economist for the insurance industry trade association, described these packaged securities: "It's not an investment product, [it's] a gambling product." And a ghoulish one at that, demonstrating the parasitic length to which Wall Street will go to make money from other peoples' money and on the backs of other peoples' risks.

* * *

As Philip Landrigan states in the *New York Times*, "In the past century, the threats to our children's health have shifted radically. Life-threatening infectious diseases—smallpox, polio, and cholera—have largely been conquered. Babies born in the United States today are expected to live two decades longer than their ancestors were 100 years ago.

"But our children are growing up in a world in which environmental toxins are ubiquitous. Measurable levels of hundreds of manmade chemicals are routinely found in the bodies of all Americans, including newborns." The latter may contact such toxins as polychlorinated biphenyls, lead, and mercury while still developing in the womb, and then get further doses through breast milk. If the infant is, by contrast, bottle fed, he or she may be exposed to phthalates (synthetics used in plastics) and bisphenol A (a hazardous resin found in plastics) in the milk bottle. These synthetics as well as lead will also be present in infants' toys. These last-named three substances have all been tied to developmental disorders.

Children nowadays are suffering higher rates of chronic disease, which have become the major causes of death and serious illness in childhood, and many scientists link this to increases in the plentitude of harmful substances to which children are exposed. Among the chronic diseases now peaking, the most common is asthma, which is up 160 percent for children under 5 since 1994, and which is firmly tied to children being exposed to cigarette smoke and air pollution.

Landrigan continues, "Chemicals called endocrine disruptors—found in pesticides, herbicides, some plastics, and air and water—can interfere with the body's hormone signaling system, potentially causing reproductive disorders, neurologic impairments, and immune dysfunction. Cancer, which kills more children under age 15 than any other disease, is linked to solvents and pesticides."

Lead, which, as noted, can already be ingested by a child in the womb, as can mercury and certain pesticides, has been linked to attention deficit disorders, autism and hyperactivity, which are now affecting a range of from 5 to 10 percent of newborns each year.

It's not as if a concerted effort to forestall these damages hasn't paid off in the past. In the 1970s, after studies revealed how lead poisoning was debilitating children, the metal was removed from gasoline and paint, producing a remarkable 90 percent drop in childhood lead poisoning. This health improvement had major repercussions economically, in that it was tied to a yearly productivity gain of $100 billion to $300 billion. And it had repercussions in terms of intelligence, with the nation's children's average IQ going up 5 to 6 points.

In the 1980s, after tests indicated that two major pesticides could retard childhood development, they were pulled out of circulation with equally positive effects.

More efforts in these directions are well worth promoting, one being the National Children's Study (NCS), a scientific program that follows U.S. children from birth to age 21, looking at how different genetic and environmental components impact on their health. Money, but not complete funding, was appropriated in 2009 to get this research rolling.

The author also names the Child Safe Chemical Act (CSCA) as "another measure that deserves support." This is a proposed law that would mandate that any new chemical being introduced to market first be evaluated and proven safe for children. Moreover, it would legislate that those chemicals now in use but untested be examined for their safety. Given that "during the past 50 years, more than 80,000 synthetic chemicals have been invented," many of which have been put into consumer products, but "most [of which] are not tested for toxicity," such a law is long overdue.

Though it has not yet been passed, this law was introduced in Congress both in 2005 and 2008, the author ends, "Our children are 30 percent of our population, but they are 100 percent of our future. They deserve our protection."

Source: *New York Times*, August 4, 2009 (by Philip Landrigan)

"This should, by all rights, be the year that Congress passes a tough chemical plant safety bill, protecting the public from one of the most serious terrorism vulnerabilities," begins a *New York Times* article on this important issue.

It continues, "There are already signs, however, that the chemical industry and its Republican allies may succeed yet again in blocking effective safety rules. The White House, which has remained in the background, needs to speak out, and Democratic leaders in Congress should work to make sure a strong bill is enacted without further delay."

The gist of the piece is that anti-terrorism experts have been proclaiming since the World Trade Center disaster that chemical plants are one of our country's most vulnerable targets, which, if effectively attacked, could "produce hundreds of thousands of deaths and injuries." Those concerned with these dangers have repeatedly spoken out on the need for stronger security measures at the plants, but in 2006 when a measure on this matter was passed, due to the intense lobbying of the chemical industry, only a defanged law was put in place.

One would think something would be done this year, given that Obama in his previous life as a senator co-sponsored a better bill, and the national legislature is filled with Democrats, who have been less beholding to the chemical industry than the Republicans, the *Times* points out. But appearance can be deceptive, and, the article says regretfully, "It is looking increasingly likely that Congress will extend the current inadequate law for another year," which leaves our country's chemical plants open invitations to any terrorists on the make.

Source: *New York Times*, August 4, 2009

Comment: Another example of Washington's regulatory tombstone mentality — waiting for a disaster to happen before acting to enact stronger laws that could have forestalled the damage. The predicted mass slaughter from sabotage of chemical plants towers over other risk scenarios that receive far more attention from the Department of Homeland Security. Chemical plant safeguards reduce accident risks and have positive environmental benefits, such as safer materials substitution and reduced exposed wastes.

According to a Congressional Research Service Report citing an EPA analysis regarding chemical plants, "at least 123 plants reported a worst-case scenario with a vulnerability zone containing more than a million people. The analysis also found that more than 700 plants could threaten 100,000 people, and at least 3,000 facilities could threaten 10,000 people in the vicinity."

* * *

It is remarkable that, for example, tens of millions of airline passengers have to lose time and convenience going through security but eight years after 9/11 the chemical industry's lobbyists have tied up Congress on a potential calamity that could take out a town or city at any one of dozens of locations around the country. These are necessary safeguards for public safety, in case of accident or negligence, apart from the matter of sabotage — long overdue.

The *Times* ran a piece in which Sarah Arnquist and Anne Underwood interviewed Victor G. Rodwin, professor of health policy and management at New York University's Wagner School of Public Service. One of his areas of study is the differences between national health systems.

When they asked him about the French health care system, which the World Health Organization in 2000 ranked as the best in the world, he replied, that the WHO evaluation should be supplemented by a second one. He continued, "A study I would take [even] more seriously is one published last year by Ellen Nolte and Martin McKee in the journal *Health Affairs*. They examined avoidable mortality—that is, deaths whose risk of occurrence would be far lower if the population had access to appropriate health care interventions."

The findings of the Nolte and McKee investigation, like that of WHO, were that France's health care system was the best, "with the lowest rate of avoidable deaths."

The fact is, he continued, France also rates at the top in "avoidable hospitalizations," that is, cases where the patient would never have needed to go to the hospital if his or her manageable health condition, such as diabetes or asthma, had not escalated because it was not properly cared for. France (as is true of Germany and Great Britain) has a low amount of such avoidable hospitalizations, particularly when compared to the U.S., which possesses an "exceedingly high rates of avoidable hospitalizations."

In France, he explains, while doctors are all private, everyone is insured by a national healthcare program, not unlike Medicare. "It's not government run but government financed." Doctors bill the government, but have autonomy, working in "office-based, fee-for service practices."

Source: *New York Times*, September 11, 2009 (Interview by Sarah Arnquist and Anne Underwood)

Comment: Comparing health statistics between two countries is always a challenge. Nonetheless, the following comparisons are noteworthy:

- Life expectancy—2009: US—79 years, France—81 years; Source: worldbank.org/
- Infant Mortality per 1,000 births—2009: US—7, France—3 Source: worldbank.org/
- Health Spending as a percentage of GDP—2008: US—16.0 France—11.2 Source: oecd.org/
- Doctors Per 10,000 people 2000-2009: US—27, France—37 Source: globalhealthfacts.org/

* * *

In her *New York Times* piece, Gretchen Morgenson remarks to the readers, "With all of the turmoil of the financial crisis, you may have forgotten about the book-cooking that went on at Fannie Mae. Government inquiries found that between 1998 and 2004, senior executives at Fannie manipulated its results to hit earnings targets and generate $115 million in bonus compensation. Fannie had to restate its financial results by $6.3 billion."

The investigation conducted into this wrongdoing, and finished in 2006, had nothing good to say about what went on. The report concluded, "The conduct of Mr. Raines, chief financial officer J. Timothy Howard, and other members of the inner circle of senior executives at Fannie Mae was inconsistent with the values of responsibility, accountability, and integrity."

To bring the top three malefactors Raines, Howard and Leanne Spencer, Fannie's former controller, to justice, the government brought suit, asking for $100 million in fines and $115 million in return for bonuses they had collected, but, the government alleged, didn't deserve. In 2008, the three anted up $31.4 million to settle the case.

Meanwhile, the trio was also faced with shareholder suits, and, ironically, Fannie Mae was contractually obligated to pay for their defense. As Morgenson states, "Those costs are ours." Taxpayers had to foot Raines $2.45 million defense, Howard's $1.35 million one, and Spencer's $2.52 million case.

Congressman Alan Grayson, who didn't appreciate the irony of the situation, spoke out, "I cannot see the justification of people who lead these organizations into insolvency getting a free ride. It goes right to the heart of what people find most disturbing in this situation—the absolute lack of justice."

Grayson added that these payments flew in the face of America's system, in which, presumably, those who do right receive benefits and those who break the law receive punishment. But here things were backward. Grayson states, in light of this, "Where is the punishment for Raines, Howard and Spencer? There is none."

Source: *New York Times*, September 6, 2009 (by Gretchen

Morgenson)

Comment: It is worse than Congressman Grayson describes. These three executives, among others, got away with tens of millions of dollars in undeserved compensation that they did not have to return during those years. And one of them, Jamie Gorelick, is not only thriving in her corporate law practice, including representing BP, but is even co-chair of the *American Bar Association's Commission on Ethics 20/20*, no less.

* * *

"What is it with these banks," Ron Lieber writes in the *Times*, "that are so quick to hit you with a fee for spending more than you have in your checking account but take their own sweet time in crediting deposits?

"My colleague Andrew Martin and I heard that complaint repeatedly from readers after we wrote about overdraft fees earlier this month." The funny thing, Lieber follows with, is that this outpouring of unhappiness comes just as the federal law, known as Check 21, is about to celebrate its fifth year. This is the statute that allowed banks to settle check transactions on computer screens, rather than, as formerly, requiring them to ship "bags of paper around the country on airplanes."

Obviously, after this change went down, banks could operate more quickly, and move money out of your account at electronic speed. But the Check 21 law left the rules about how speedily a bank must credit any deposit you make just as they had been, allowing them to continue to hit you with fees for being overdrawn at the old time rate. This is another double standard that allows the banks to play by new rules while forcing their customers to abide by laws that "haven't changed in more than 20 years."

Source: *New York Times*, September 9, 2009 (by Ron Lieber)

"Many credit card users are in a panic as lenders snatch away long-held but unused credit cards or significantly reduce their available credit lines."

According to *Washington Post* writer Michelle Singletary, these losses or reductions can easily end with the affected person getting a lower credit score. And as the score goes down, it costs more to borrow money and insurance rates go up.

On the other hand, these changes may cause people to rely less on credit, which may help them keep their finances in order.

Source: *Washington Post*, April 30, 2009 (by Michelle Singletary)

Comment: Note how powerless credit card holders can be against those mysterious credit-scoring algorithms created by unaccountable unknown companies such as Fair Isaac Corp.

* * *

"T-Mobile USA has dropped a plan to begin charging its customers $1.50 per month to get a paper copy of their bill in the mail." So opens a trenchant piece in the *Wall Street Journal*, which goes on to note that after the company told its subscribers of this planned new fee, it had to back down after "an outcry from customers and threats of legal action."

The original idea was anyone who didn't sign up for paperless billing, conducted via the Internet, would have to begin forking over the new payment.

New York Attorney General Andrew Cuomo was displeased, noting that it was not within the company's rights to tack on a new charge without previously giving its customers the choice of opting out of contracts which, as originally written, included no such fee.

Source: *Wall Street Journal*, September 16, 2009 (from the Associated Press)

Comment: T-Mobile's customers are charged $3.49 a month to be able to check the billing for each call and see if there were mistakes or overcharges. Another example of corporate domination, backed up by penalties for quitting T-Mobile early.

* * *

A recent study done by the Associated Press looked into how multinationals were promoting the sale of their infant formulas in Vietnam, and came to the troubling conclusion that they had no compunction about bending or breaking the country's law, which had been engineered to promote breast feeding.

As Ben Stocking put it in the *Washington Post*, "International guidelines and Vietnamese law recognize breast milk as superior to formula for an infant's health. Yet dozens of interviews with mothers, doctors, health officials and shopkeepers suggest that formula companies promote their products for infants less than a year old, approach mothers and health-care workers at health facilities, and pay doctors to peddle formula—all of which are against the law.

"The number of Vietnamese mothers who exclusively breast-feed in the first six-months after their babies are born—the most crucial period—stands at 17 percent, less than half what it was a decade ago, according to UNICEF." While breastfeeding is dramatically decreasing, formula sales are taking off, having risen 39 percent in 2008. That figure is the result of an investigation by market research firm Nielsen. A different study looked into the infant formula companies' marketing costs in the Southeast Asian nation, and learned the industry laid out $10 million on advertising last year, securing it a place among the nation's five biggest advertisers.

These results don't bode well for the government's plans, announced during World Breastfeeding Week, to achieve a "50 percent exclusive breast-feeding rate by 2015."

Annelies Allain of the International Code Documentation Center said that the situation was bleak. "The companies have millions of dollars and dozens of lawyers, but the Vietnamese government has a tiny budget and just two people promoting breast-feeding."

Source: *Washington Post*, September 20, 2009 (by Ben Stocking of the Associated Press)

Comment: Using infant formula is not just detracting from a better breastfeeding regime. Because of its expense, poor mothers often dilute the instant formula to stretch its volume. Often the water is contaminated. In 1981, the World Health Organization estimated one million child deaths a year due to diarrhea and other ailments from contaminated infant formula.

* * *

David S. Hilzenrath, examining documents made public by a California advocacy group, writes in the *Washington Post* that if a proposed law were passed that would forbid companies from taking into consideration preexisting conditions when writing insurance, this would not only be a boon, as most acknowledge, to those in poor health, but, it turns out, also to the healthy.

The revelations contained in the released documents indicate some insurance companies recommend their staff deny coverage to those with such seemingly innocuous conditions as acne, hemorrhoids and bunions.

Hilzenrath continues, "One big insurer refused to issue individual policies to police officers and firefighters, along with people in other hazardous occupations.

"Some treated pregnancy or the intention to adopt as a reason for rejection. ...

"A PacifiCare 'Medical Underwriting Guidelines' document from 2003 lists under 'Ineligible Occupations' such risk-takers as stunt people, test pilots and circus workers—along with police officers, firefighters and migrant workers."

And that's not an end to the conditions that can block you from getting coverage. Being pregnant or an "expectant father" are two more that may stop the insurer from taking you on as is having seen a therapist within six months of applying. And, then, there's the all-purpose reason for barring applicants: "currently experiencing/ experienced within the last 12 months symptoms for which a physician has not been consulted."

With so many restrictions, it's a surprise anyone can get medical insurance.

Source: *Washington Post*, September 19, 2009 (by David S.

Hilzenrath)

Comment: The new Health Insurance Reform law, passed in 2010, is supposed to prohibit preexisting conditions as grounds for health insurance companies denying coverage. It will take not take effect until 2014 and insurers may yet find ways to circumvent or avoid such bans. Looking back, consider the anguish, pain and insecurity that have been inflicted on tens of millions of Americans and their families due to inability to get health insurance even when able to pay for it. Canadians and western Europeans, who live in countries that insure their people from the moment they are born, because they are human beings, shake their heads in disbelief at the permitted callousness and greed of these companies in the U.S.A.

* * *

For all its negative features, New York City Mayor Bloomberg's administration has been on the forefront in advocating healthy eating as evidenced in such programs as banning trans fats in restaurants, asking neighborhood mini-marts to carry low-fat milk and greens, and trying to get more fresh fruit sold in poor areas.

Now, he is pushing, as Diane Cardwell writes in the *New York Times*, "to establish an even bigger beachhead for health food—new supermarkets in areas where fresh produce is scarce and where poverty, obesity and diabetes run high."

Cardwell explains, "Under a proposal the City Planning Commission unanimously approved on Wednesday, the city would offer zoning and tax incentives to spur the development of full-service grocery stores that devote a certain amount of space to fresh produce, meat, dairy and other perishables."

The idea is that by giving them tax breaks and the right to ignore certain features of zoning laws, the city could encourage developers to build supermarkets in such underserved communities as "swaths of northern Manhattan, central Brooklyn and the South Bronx, as well as downtown Jamaica in Queens."

Amanda M. Burden, the city planning commissioner, said, at the moment, in these neglected parts of the city, residents use "their grocery dollars at Duane Reade and CVS on chips and soda." The new plan would make available fresh produce and other, healthier eatables in places now without them.

Source: *New York Times*, September 24, 2009 (by Diane Cardwell)

Comment: Imagine just how disintegrated these populous communities have become that City Hall has to use many taxpayer dollars to subsidize companies to locate and sell to desiring consumers who have been abandoned for decades. Back in the early 20th century, poor communities always had grocery stores selling fresh produce along with grocery carts on street-corners everywhere. This was an era before fast food, the dominance of denuded, sugared, salted, fat-saturated processed foods, snacks and chemical agriculture. City Hall did not have to bribe them to be there. Regress replacing progress.

* * *

A recent case history, reported by Nicholas D. Kristof in the *New York Times*, is the story of "M.," a woman forced to make a difficult decision due to the irrationality of our healthcare system.

The story is that her husband has been deteriorating mentally as he has aged, and she realized that at some point she wouldn't be able to take care of him and would have to place him in an institution. She considered her options and talked to a social worker, "who outlined how the dementia and its financial toll on the family would progress, and then added, out of the blue: 'Maybe you should divorce.'

"'I was blown away,' M. told me. But, she said, the hospital staff members explained that they had seen it all before, many times. If M's husband required long-term care, the costs would be catastrophic even for a middle-class family with savings."

What would eventually happen, the social worker said, was that everything she and her husband had saved would be lost, including their retirement nest egg and money they had meant to pass on to their children. Only after they had exhausted all that money could they go on Medicaid. The single way to stave off this financial disaster would be for her to break up with her husband.

After frantically looking around for other means of escaping financial ruin, M. followed the way laid out for her by the social worker. As she told Kristof, "It took about a year for me to do the divorce, it was so hard."

She has continued to live with, care for and worry about her ex-husband, and she also worries about being found out in that she lied in claiming she wanted a divorce for "irreconcilable differences." The true reason behind her change in marital status was "because of irreconcilable medical bills."

Source: *New York Times*, August 30, 2009 (by Nicholas D. Kristof)

Comment: Another American nightmare that leaves Western Europeans' heads shaking. Steaming more?

* * *

A *Wall Street Journal* piece written by Gary Locke, the U.S. Secretary of Commerce, is an incisive commentary on how our out-of-control medical system adversely affects not only the hapless people who get ensnared in one of its dilemmas, such as M., discussed in the last selection, but businesses as well. Locke begins, "Rising health-care costs are crushing American companies—particularly small businesses that are the source of much of our economic vitality."

He notes that the price firms pay for health insurance for their workers is astronomical, having risen from the 1.2 percent of their payroll they had to pay in 1960, to the nearly 10 percent they had to plunk down in 2006. With such high costs, ones greater than what most foreign firms pay, it is difficult for U.S. companies to compete in the global marketplace or hire more workers.

After these remarks, Locke hones in on the plight of small businesses. These are the companies, which, unable to rely on the economy of scale and so get the cheaper insurance rates large firms can find, "on average, pay 8 percent more per worker than large firms for a smaller risk pool." In counting the cost, it's necessary to add to that the fact that small business ends up paying higher "administrative costs per worker" and heftier brokerage fees. Given how such burdens accrue to those small businesses offering health plans to workers, many chose not to. In 2008, 51 percent of firms with three to nine workers didn't offer coverage, though the situation improved for those companies with between 10 to 24 employees. Of these, 78 percent offer coverage. However, it is the larger concerns, those with 200 or above workers, which could really afford the coverage. A full 99 percent of such firms offered employee plans.

Locke also goes into how "the pernicious price of run-away health-care costs also has a dampening effect on entrepreneurship."

He's not talking about the discouragingly high price a small business start up would have to pay to offer employees health insurance, but that many are afraid to strike out on their own and give up jobs in workplaces where they are securely covered by their company's plan, and begin their own businesses while having to pay their own large health insurance premiums or forego insurance altogether.

Source: *Wall Street Journal*, August 22, 2009 (by Gary Locke, U.S. Secretary of Commerce)

Jim Dwyer, in a *New York Times* piece, had a mouthful to say about how credit card companies have been using introductory offers to lure in new customers then hitting them with higher rates once they are hooked.

Dwyer illustrates with the example of Medgar Evers college student Malcolm S, who picked up a new card around Thanksgiving 2008. He felt lucky to get one with a bargain interest rate of 2 percent. He could use it because he was handling business for his nursing-home-bound grandfather.

Before he knew it, he had $2,000 in charges, and the low interest rate was long gone. With the higher rate and other fees, $2,000 had become $4,300, and Malcolm S was in court, sued by the credit card company when he couldn't pay.

Dwyer notes, "The interest rate was around 29 percent. The judge, Noach Dear, held his head. 'John Gotti must be looking down and smiling,' Judge Dear said. 'Even he wouldn't have the chutzpah to charge that interest.'"

The back story to such examples of usurious rates is filled in by Dwyer in the following. "Between 1978 and 1980, the banking industry was effectively liberated from limits on the interest that could be charged on loans, including credit cards. A Supreme Court decision and federal legislation overrode most state laws that defined and prohibited usury. A new world of payday loans, tax refund loans, subprime mortgages and teaser-rate credit cards was born, just as real hourly wages, adjusted for inflation, were stagnating. It took three decades for the country to borrow and lend its way into a global financial collapse."

The situation is so out of hand that representatives from the Industrial Areas Foundation, a national organizing network, recently met to discuss how to bring these excessive rates down.

Mike Gecan, a senior organizer in the I.A.F., said that controls of interest rates have a long historical pedigree. He added, "There's nothing new about speed limits on roads, either."

Source: *New York Times*, November 25, 2009 (by Jim Dwyer)

Comment: The banking and credit card lobbies were instrumental in getting rid of the state usury laws.

* * *

A *New York Times* editorial entitled "Taming the Fat Cats," begins by remarking on how President Obama has shared the concerns of average Americans about the recent outrageous behavior of bankers, who after receiving the benefits of government largesse to save them from financial ruin, turned around and offered little in return. They have been withholding credit from American business while being very forthcoming when it comes to "multibillion-dollar bonuses" for their own executives.

The editorial then lays out how the British have dealt with the spectacle of such lavish, and often unearned perks. They have slapped "a hefty windfall tax on their [bankers'] bonuses."

It's not as if the government, which could use the tax money so accrued, didn't deserve it. It's a case of tit for tat. The government propped up the banks when they were in financial peril, so why shouldn't it get back its own bonus now that these firms are back on their feet and cashing in?

As the piece concludes, "We can think of a lot of good ways to use the revenue from a windfall tax, starting with a more robust program to create jobs for out-of-work Americans. ...

"A windfall tax on bankers' bonuses would not be enough, but it would be a start. The government also needs to ensure that all banks reform their compensation practices to better align rewards with performance, good and bad. That is the best hope for curbing bankers' unbridled appetite for risk."

Source: *New York Times,* December 20, 2009 (editorial)

"History will record the third week of March 2009 as Outrage Week in Washington," according to Joel Achenbach, writing for the *Washington Post.*

Outrage One, he notes, came when news appeared of million-dollar bonuses going to executives at AIG, a company that had lately been preserved from ruin by a U.S. government bailout. Sensing the voters' outrage, both parties in Congress got together and passed "a punitive 90 percent tax on the bonuses."

Outrage Two, or Counter Outrage, appeared as many Washington-based pundits and commentators tongue-lashed Congress for giving in to mob rule without taking time to think through what they were doing.

What Achenbach wonders about, though, is the question: What made this particular outrage (number 1), after months of similar outrages, arouse the public. After all, why did this (comparatively) paltry $165 million in bonuses "roil the capital so feverishly after months of the government shoveling tens of billions, hundreds of billions, make that trillions of dollars, to private companies?"

Achenbach guesses these bonuses are the famed *camel-back-breaking straw*, which is causing citizens to either scratch their heads or raise their fists.

As one interviewed worker, a sanitation man, Ricardo Brandon, complained, "We're doing labor. We get a bonus, we get, like, 50 cents." And as 25 year-old Daisy Montague put it more angrily, "I think those folks are basically stealing from taxpayers such as myself."

Neil Pfortsch, 51, a concrete pump operator, also interviewed, said the AIG execs shouldn't be getting big payouts but should be doing big time at the big house. In his words, "They ought to put 'em in jail."

Tyler Gilbert, 33, a real estate consultant with a lot of mouths to feed, a family of five, stated succinctly, "Something's gotta change, and something's gotta change quick,"

Source: *Washington Post*, March 22, 2009 (by Joel Achenbach)

Comment: The outrage-driven House bill to tax these bonuses at a 90 percent rate was sent to the Senate graveyard and has not been heard from since. Obama did not explicitly support it either. Washington outrage is a highly depreciable commodity when there is no organized citizen base back home to turn outrage into legislative justice. So sorry, Mr. Gilbert, "something's not gonna change," so long as tens of millions of people like you keep taking it on the chin and keep rationalizing their own futility vis-à-vis only 535 men and women in Congress who put their shoes on every day like we do.

* * *

Previewing a report that was to come out from the Commodity Futures Trading Commission, Ianthe Dugan and Alistain McDonald in the *Wall Street Journal*, note that it will emphasize that "speculators played a significant role in driving wild swings in oil prices—a reversal of an earlier CFTC position that augurs intensifying scrutiny on investors."

In its first report, the agency, which is "the main U.S. futures-market regulator," argued that price fluctuations were nothing more than a manifestation of the laws of supply and demand. This corrected report is appearing because, as one of the four CFTC commissioners, Bart Chilton, stated, report number one was based on "deeply flawed data."

This revised version could be a sign of a new CFTC regime, which, under a different director, Obama appointee Gary Gensler, is giving more intense scrutiny to futures trading. Evidence of this proactive approach should appear shortly as the agency is mulling plans to limit "the amount of investments in commodities by big institutions betting on their direction purely for financial gain."

Such new regulations are being pushed by many legislators who are worried that if unrestrained speculation on such common consumer items as "heating oil, food and other essentials" is allowed to continue, the average American will be hurt in the pocketbook. North Dakota Democrat Byron Dorgan is one of those prodding the agency to adopt tougher regulations, noting that we have to control "oil speculators looking for a quick buck at the expense of American consumers."

Source: *Wall Street Journal*, July 28, 2009 (by Ianthe Dugan and Alistain McDonald)

Comment: The report was never issued, but the CFTC does now regularly release more detailed data on trading.

* * *

Recent events in Japan have made all to clear the dangers of reliance on nuclear power for energy, but the reactors used to provide this power have been beset with problems all along. In May 2009, Matthew L. Wald did a piece for the *New York Times*, where he talked about problems at Indian Point 2 nuclear plant in Buchanan, N.Y., in which the appearance of water in one of the buildings was traced to a leak in a buried pipe, leading to "concern about the plant's underground pipes and those of other aging reactors across the country."

Wald notes further, "A one-and-a-half-inch hole caused by corrosion allowed about 108,000 gallons of water to escape from the main system that keeps that reactor cool immediately after any shutdown, according to nuclear experts. The leak was discovered on February 16, according to the plant's owner, Entergy Nuclear Northeast, a subsidiary of the Entergy Corporation.

"Entergy and the federal Nuclear Regulatory Commission emphasized that the Indian Point reactor could still have been shut down safely with either of two other backup systems, although operators generally avoid using both."

Still, it was hardly reassuring to learn that the system that would cool the reactors was disabled by a leak in *one* buried pipe. Both the company and the regulatory commission are studying how this happened.

More particularly, they are examining what seems to be a newly revealed vulnerability, the "decades-old buried pipes at the nation's nuclear plants." These could be weak links, ones that are not being evaluated as they age. For instance, the underground part of "neither the eight-inch supply pipe nor the 12-inch pipe connecting the tank to the reactor cooling system," which caused the problem at Indian Point, have been looked at since they day they were laid back in August 1973. And the Nuclear Regulatory Commission, apparently assuming nothing can go wrong, does not require plants to eyeball hidden pipes.

This leak is one reason many are calling for the plant to be decommissioned when its license runs out in 2013. For instance, the chair of the House subcommittee on energy and the environment, Edward J. Markey, says this leak suggests the company and the regulatory commission are very careless watchdogs of the plant's safety.

"This leak may demonstrate a systemic failure of the licensee and the commission to inspect critical buried pipes in a manner sufficient to guarantee the public health and safety," he wrote to the commission.

Underground pipes have been overlooked as potential sources of trouble, but now "buried pipes are emerging as endemic problems as reactors age." Even so, till now most attention has been paid to what might leak out instead of to the equally serious issue of how to handle these pipes as they inevitably wear out.

Source: *New York Times*, May 4, 2009 (by Matthew L. Wald)

Comment: The Indian Point nuclear plants are 26 miles from New York City. A class nine nuclear meltdown—the worse-case scenario—whether through accident or sabotage, could contaminate the living and working space of many millions of people with untold casualties and cancer epidemics. That is one reason critics of nuclear power have said that this technology has just one bite of the apple.

* * *

Kate Bronfenbrenner wrote an op-ed piece for the *Washington Post*, which she began with this vignette: "Angel Warner, an employee at a Rite Aid distribution center, sat next to me recently in a congressional briefing room and described what happened when she and her fellow workers tried to form a union in their California workplace. She talked about the surveillance, constant threats and harassment they endured; how she and other workers were repeatedly taken aside and interrogated, one on one, about how they planned to vote; how two co-workers were fired; and how the rest lived in fear that any day they, too, might get a pink slip."

The union fought back by filing suit against the company for these blatant union-busting efforts and won the right to hold an election, but even after three years of fighting, the Rite Aide union's members are without a contract.

This is no isolated example, the author notes. Current labor law hamstrings workers who want to form a new union or carry out collective bargaining. And companies have taken full cognizance of this situation, exploiting every nuance of the weak law which, in Bronfenbrenner's words, "neither protect workers' rights nor provide disincentives for employers to stop disregarding those rights."

This slanting of the balance of power against workers is hardly a carryover from the old days, for, as a study by the writer and others at the *Post* has has indicated, workers' rights have been continually diminished in the last two decades. Indeed, these rights have plummeted in the last decade.

Her studies show that employers are twice as likely now as they were as recently as the 1990s to use 10 or more tactics to ward off workers' unionization drives. Even more chilling, management has come to rely on more aggressive methods, including firing militants and threatening the shutdown of plants, over less coercive ones, used formerly, such as offering cosmetic improvements, to accomplish its goal of having a union-free environment.

Bronfenbrenner ends with the warning that "unless Congress passes serious labor law reform with real penalties," there is little hope that workers who want to form unions will be able to do so, for "there will no longer be a functioning legal mechanism to effectively protect the right of private-sector workers to organize and collectively bargain."

Source: *Washington Post*, June 3, 2009 (an op-ed by Kate Bronfenbrenner, director of labor education research at Cornell University's School of Industrial and Labor Relations)

In a story datelined Rocky Mount, N.C., writer Kevin Sack brings great empathy to his *New York Times* report of how the high cost of American pharmaceuticals combined with the economic downturn are being played out in this medium-sized city in the U.S.

Visiting Almand's Drug Store, he learned that maybe a year ago customers buying pharmaceuticals were most concerned about side effects and the right doses, but now their tunes have changed. Their only interest is price.

As he writes, he couldn't help but overhear a woman asking the druggist about her anti-depressant Lexapro, "Can I get this as a generic? Is the co-pay really that high? Will you match WalMart's $4 price?"

She ended up bargaining, "Can I just have four pills until payday on Friday?"

This is the reality here and across America as customers, no longer able to afford the stiff prices, can only manage to buy a portion of the drugs their doctors prescribe.

Even in the face of various measures that have lowered cost, such as Medicare's drug benefits and the fact that many common prescription drugs are available as generics, more and more Americans are finding, with their tightened belts, that they can't replenish supplies of needed drugs.

A doctor who works in a low-income clinic near the Rocky Mount pharmacy, John T. Avent, says he's finding the bulk of his patients, up to 80 percent, can't afford all their prescribed medicines.

When he sees a patient with blood pressure problems, for instance, the man will tell him he hasn't kept up with his medication for the past month. Dr. Avent continued, "By that time, of course, [his] blood pressure is highly elevated and hemoglobin AIC is two to three times what it should be."

Another doctor, Daniel C. Miniork, who is in charge of the emergency department at Nash General, said he saw the same situation among patients coming to the hospital. They didn't have their jobs anymore and so they couldn't come up with cash to pay for their pills. Most shocking to him is that "it's even occurring among younger and working-age people. That's not something we saw before."

Source: *New York Times*, June 4, 2009 (by Kevin Sack)

"It was called the 'Homeland Investment Act,'" states Floyd Norris in the *New York Times*. This law "was sold to Congress as a way to spur investment in America, building plants, increasing research and development and creating jobs. It gave international companies a large one-time tax break on overseas profits, but only if the money was used for specific job-building investments in the United States.

"The law specifically said the money could not be used to raise dividends or to repurchase shares."

That, at least, was how the whole thing was billed and sold in 2004, according to Norris, but now a "detailed analysis of what actually happened—using confidential government data as well as corporate reports"—shows that most of the money, 92 percent of the $299 billion in repatriated profits, did exactly what the law nominally prohibited it from doing, that is, was turned over to shareholders in larger dividends or through other means. So, simply put, almost none of it was spent doing what it was mandated to do, provide jobs, fund research or act in other ways to boost U.S. business investment and job creation.

The study of what turned out to be the abject failure of the Homeland Investment Act was carried out by three economists, including one who had worked on the original bill. This former Bush official, Ms. Forbes, said, "Repatriations did not lead to an increase in domestic investment, employment or R&D, even for the firms that lobbied for the tax holiday stating these intentions."

In case after case, she explained, the intent of the law was forgotten as soon as the companies got their hands on the money.

She gave the example of Dell Computer. "They lobbied very hard for the tax holiday. They said part of the money would be brought back to build a new plant in Winston-Salem, N.C. They did bring back $4 billion, and spent $100 million on the plant, which they admitted would have been built anyway. About two months after that, they used $2 billion for a share buyback."

Source: *New York Times*, June 4, 2009 (by Floyd Norris)

Comment: Corporations can promise to secure huge monetary rewards, break their promise and still get away with it, as they go after the next tax break. Do you think individuals, no matter how rich, could have gotten away with this privilege and immunity?

This jobs creation act was supposed to induce the investment of these networked foreign profits in American job creation by sharply reducing taxes. Instead these companies broke this understanding and put over 90 percent of the money into stock buybacks, dividends and acquisitions. So much for these "corporate promises."

* * *

"The poorer you are, the more things cost. More in money, time, hassle, exhaustion, menace. This is a fact of life that reality television and magazines don't often explain." So begins a heartfelt article in the *Washington Post* by Deneen Brown.

She zeroes in on financial services as one instance of this discrepancy. "The rich have direct deposit for their paychecks." Poorer people end up standing in line at check-cashing storefronts to convert their paychecks into cash.

Credit, too, is not easily obtained, and, if it is found, it's usually at places such as "First Cash Advance in D.C.'s Manor Park neighborhood, where a neon sign once flashed 'PAYDAY ADVANCE.'"

Here, if you could convince the cashier you were creditworthy by flashing a pay stub, checkbook and ID, you might get a $300 loan. The interest on that loan would be $46.50. And that's for holding the money for one week! That works out to a yearly rate of 806 percent. Even Shylock would have been ashamed to ask for that.

Source: *Washington Post*, May 18, 2009 (by Deneen L. Brown)

We saw a moment ago how the government was finagled via the Homeland Investment Act to allow companies to repatriate profits at a low rate under false pretenses. That's not the only way big companies have found to use foreign assets to their advantage when it comes to taxes.

A case recently reported by Jesse Drucker in the *Wall Street Journal* focuses on GlaxoSmithKline PLC, which "is embroiled in a potential $1.9 billion court battle with the Internal Revenue Service, which says the drug-maker owes back taxes, interest and penalties stemming from tax deductions generated essentially by making payments to itself."

The way that worked is through a device known as "earnings stripping." By this method, a multinational company can lower its U.S. taxes by making deductions based on payments it made to one of its foreign branches. As if by magic, while its taxes are cut down or eliminated, no money has actually left the company—it has merely been transferred from one unit to another—while the firm's "publicly reported profit is unchanged."

Earnings stripping is of acute concern to the U.S. government in that, as Reuven Avi-Yonah, director of the international-tax program at the University of Michigan Law School, notes, this practice "significantly reduces the U.S. corporate-tax base."

What the courts decide in this case will have repercussions far beyond the ultimate fate of GlaxoSmithKline's ability to take a deduction. As H. David Rosenbloom, tax attorney at Caplin & Drysdale, remarked, "People will pay attention to this, because there are plenty of people who have done similar transactions."

Source: *Wall Street Journal*, May 23, 2009 (by Jesse Drucker)

Comment: Attorney Rosenbloom really meant "corporations" when he said "people." People, no matter how extended their family business may be around the world, cannot get away with such self-defining tax escapes. The Glaxo/IRS case is worth pondering.

* * *

"The question at the heart of one of the biggest Supreme Court cases this year is simple: What constitutional rights should corporations have? To us, as well as many legal scholars, former justices and, indeed, drafters of the Constitution, the answer is that their rights should be quite limited—far less than those of people.

"This Supreme Court, the John Roberts court, seems to be having trouble with that. It has been on a campaign to increase corporations' legal rights—based on the conviction of some conservative justices that businesses are, at least legally, not much different than people. ...

The legal doctrine underlying this debate is known as 'corporate personhood.'"

Going into the historical background, this *Times* editorial notes corporations have long had certain privileges that are possessed by human individuals, such as the right to sue, to enter into contracts, and own property, but have not been able to do everything people can. Since 1907, for instance, the country has "banned them from contributing to federal political campaigns—a ban the Supreme Court has repeatedly upheld."

This ban fits in with the generally skeptical attitude toward corporations evinced by both the Constitution and such notable chief justices as John Marshall, perhaps our nation's greatest, the editorial continues.

After all, under law, corporations also possess certain rights people do not have, including, "limited liability, special rules for the accumulation of assets and the ability to live forever." These special allowances give them means to acquire wealth superior to that possessed by individuals, which could allow them undue influence on democratic government if they could legally become involved in elections.

This danger is well appreciated by the average American citizen, as revealed in recent polls, but not attended to by the Supreme Court's conservative bloc, who, while constantly proclaiming their adherence to the Constitution, seem to fly in the face of that document's actual import. As the editorial ends, "The founders of this nation knew just what they were doing when they drew a line between legally created economic entities and living, breathing human beings. The court should stick to that line."

Source: *New York Times*, September 22, 2009 (Editorial, "The Rights of Corporations")

Comment: On January 21, 2010, the Supreme Court, by a vote of five to four, ruled that corporations can spend unlimited money for or against any candidates for electoral office as long as such money is independently expended. (*Citizens United vs. Federal Election Commission*. 558 U.S. 50 (2010))

* * *

"Wall Street, Sand Hill Road, LaSalle Street: some corporate addresses scream money. Then there is North Orange Street, which whispers it.

"North Orange, a ho-hum thoroughfare in Wilmington, Delaware, is, on paper, home to more than 6,500 companies. Many of them are empty shells. They make nothing and sometimes employ just a lone clerk. But all are there for the same reason: to help corporations avoid paying taxes in other states."

Just as many corporations use the Cayman Islands and other tax havens to avoid paying their fair share, so, as Lynnley Browning reports in this *New York Times* article, many are now shifting to Delaware for the same reason. This placing of corporate shells in Delaware has recently accelerated in that "squeezed by hard times, states are pushing to collect taxes," which previously they let slide.

A good example of this new tax-hunting drive is Maryland, which recently collected $267 million, "including interest and penalties," from delinquent firms, and is dunning the corporate sector for a further $143 million.

Delaware's place in this scheme of things as an asylum for firms looking to escape taxation has many critics, such as George Washington University School of Law professor David E. Brunori, who sounded off, saying that moving nominal offices to Delaware "is a vehicle for avoiding otherwise legitimate tax liabilities at a time when states need money badly."

Source: *New York Times*, May 30, 2009 (by Lynnley Browning)

A piece by Philip Rucker and Joe Stephens in the *Washington Post* casts a harsh light on the prevailing practice of financial regulators or others in government posts receiving high fees from the very companies they are overseeing.

Case in point, "Lawrence H. Summers, one of President Obama's top economic advisers, collected roughly $5.2 million in compensation from hedge fund D.E. Shaw over the past year and was paid more than $2.7 million in speaking fees by several troubled Wall Street firms and other organizations." His list of paymasters included JP Morgan Chase, Citigroup, Goldman Sachs, Lehman Brothers and Merrill Lynch, who all wanted him to give speeches. His words don't come cheap. He netted $45,000 for a Merrill Lynch appearance and $135,000 from Goldman Sachs. Summers, as the writers remind us, "as chairman of the National Economic Council, is a leading architect of the administration's economic policies and helped shape the response to the global recession."

Receiving such corporate largesse is the norm nowadays. Not doing as well but still making a handsome showing last year was National security advisor James L. Jones, who picked up $900,000 in salary from the U.S. Chamber of Commerce, $1.1 million from five corporations, "including defense contractor Boeing," and hundreds of thousands for acting as a corporate consultant.

Source: *Washington Post*, April 4, 2009 (by Philip Rucker and Joe Stephens)

Comment: Not exactly the man for "hope and change" that Obama voters expected to reform Wall Street greed and power that cost millions of jobs and trillions of pension and savings dollars.

* * *

"Good old K Street, where the big tea party never stopped, has all but halted organized labor's effort to make it easier for workers to unionize," writes Thomas Frank in another of his acerbic pieces for the *Wall Street Journal*.

The point at issue is the Employee Free Choice Act (EFCA), a bill which would have made it easier to organize unions, and which, after a lobbying battle between labor, which was fighting for the bill's passage, and business interests, which opposed it, has little chance of passage in that it can't muster the 60 votes that would be able to break a promised filibuster by Senate Republicans.

This promised defeat is especially dispiriting because organized labor went all out to put Obama in the White House with a friendly Democratic congress to stand behind him. But even with these wins, to which labor contributed mightily, it seems, as happened in parallel cases under Jimmy Carter and Bill Clinton, who also profited from labor's electoral support, the unions' efforts will receive little reward.

As Frank ends, "Why does labor always get it in the neck?"

Source: *Wall Street Journal*, April 22, 2009 (by Thomas Frank)

Comment: Neither the Democratic President nor the Democratic Congress has bothered even to formally propose and have hearings on EFCA, although the President and the Party formally endorsed these labor reform at numerous public events during the 2008 presidential campaign.

* * *

"The consumer nightmare of the moment," according to a Jonathan D. Glater piece in the *New York Times*, is this: "You try to get cash from an ATM and discover that your money is gone, seized under a court order that you never knew about."

How could such an event transpire, one that has "happened to thousands of people across New York—and potentially tens of thousands more across the country?" It's the result of the consumer having been summoned to a debt collections legal hearing, and not showing up because the individual never got notification of the proceedings.

Glater continues, "The attorney general, Andrew M. Cuomo, plans to file a civil suit Tuesday against one such company, American Legal Process of Lynbrook, N.Y.," which is suspected of being a company that is not delivering the legal notifications for which it has taken responsibility. American Legal is one of the country's largest in the field, and so its dereliction is all the more worrying.

When a person is summoned to court by a debtor, he or she then has the possibility of disputing the claims of owing money. Yet, not many chose to make a court appearance in such cases, "fewer than 10 percent," in fact, according to a study by MFY Legal Services.

One reason the appearance rate is so low may be that people don't know what's going on. Since the fee for delivering a notice is as miniscule as $5 a pop, it's tempting, according to Ms. Coffey, a lawyer with MFY, for the one bringing the notification to practice "sewer service," discarding the document in the sewer while claiming the supposed recipient has the notice in hand.

Coffey stated that if you do learn that a notification has gone astray, you can "challenge an adverse judgment" by going to court and arguing that the notice informing you of the case never reached you. Still, she noted, "You shouldn't have to do that."

Source: *New York Times*, April 4, 2009 (by Jonathan D. Glater)

Comment: Sewer service was exposed by consumer groups, and the New York City media over forty years ago. Still it continues. The powerful New York City Bar Associations have not seen fit to work to stop this basic denial of due process which amounts to criminal fraud on unknowing, often low income, defendants.

* * *

"Hospitals are turning to a new breed of antibiotic SWAT team to win the war against 'superbugs,' the bacteria that are outmaneuvering nearly every weapon in the arsenal of drugs long used to fight them," reports Laura Landro in the *Wall Street Journal*.

She suggests that it's possible to account for the introduction of these more aggressive programs by the fact that the federal Medicare program has decided it will no longer pay for the treatment of infections acquired at the hospital as well as because of the proliferation of hospital-acquired infections. About two million people get these infections every year, to which some 90,000 succumb.

The most dangerous of these illnesses are those due to superbugs, such as "the current epidemic of MRSA," an extraordinarily potent and drug resistant staph infection that is being found in hospitals and locker rooms.

The groups brought in to wage war on these infections, are "known as anti-microbial stewardship programs, team top pharmacists, infectious-disease specialists and microbiologists." Their charge is to watch over how a hospital is administering antibiotics, immediately curtailing the use of any which germs seem to be learning to withstand. Two "leading hospital purchasing groups" are already onboard in this new effort.

Source: *Wall Street Journal*, April 3, 2009 (by Laura Landro)

Comment: 90,000 preventable deaths annually in the U.S. is about equal to thirty 9/11s every year. The above report is laudable but what took these hospitals so long? For decades overuse of antibiotics, pushed by drug companies and prescribed by physicians creating lethal bacteria resistance has been reported in medical journals, magazines and newspapers. Without powerful organized consumers (patients), this enormous number of preventable fatalities has continued year after year.

* * *

As just noted, hospitals increasingly have to deal with bacterial infections that are resistant to most current antibiotics. They are also facing a dramatic number of patients with "food-borne illnesses." Some of these "illnesses are on the upswing, giving new urgency to efforts to reform the nation's food safety system, the Centers for Disease Control and Prevention reported yesterday," as Lyndsey Layton writes in the *Washington Post*.

She quotes Robert Tauxe, deputy director of the CDC's Division of Food-Borne, Bacterial and Mycotic Diseases, who states, "We need greater effort at all stages of movement of food in the food chain from farm to table" in order to get a handle on this health hazard.

He points to a number of reasons food-borne sicknesses are getting out of control. These include "the intricacy of the U.S. food chain, the changing nature of the contaminating bacteria and the rise in imported food," Particularly alarming among new findings on these illnesses is that some bacteria, ones which used to be found exclusively in meat, have now migrated to produce. As illustrations of this new trend, he cited "E. coli 0157 in spinach, and salmonella in peanuts and pistachios."

The situation is hardly helped by the fact that the Food and Drug Administration, whose responsibility it is to keep tabs on the safety of our nation's food, is generally short on money and personnel.

Last year, the Government Accountability Office looked into how the agency was dealing with the new threat posed by germs in produce and found "the FDA provided little or no oversight," not even inspecting 1 percent of fresh produce that came into the country between 2002 and 2007, nor was it looking into new germs such as E. coli 0157, because there were no funds for research.

Its incapacity was underlined by the outbreak of "salmonella illness linked to peanuts." This caused great public alarm, something which spurred politicians to take action, with Obama vowing to reform the FDA, making it more scrupulous, and with lawmakers putting forward a half dozen bills that would better food safety requirements.

Source: *Washington Post*, April 10, 2009 (by Lyndsey Layton)

Comment: The FDA is greatly underfunded, has very weak enforcement authority and is hampered by corporate lobbyists who have stalled food safety legislation for years while over 5,000 Americans die and tens of millions are sickened annually from contaminated food. To starve the FDA and pour tens of billions of tax dollars into weapons systems that retired generals and admirals say we do not need is not rational. It is criminogenic.

* * *

The weakness of labor on many fronts, already chronicled in these pages, was addressed in a *New York Times* editorial, which turned to "an unfinished labor battle from the New Deal."

Looking backward, the author outlines that in the 1930s when many labor reforms were pressed through by the Roosevelt Administration, the government drew a line at offering protection to farm and domestic workers. Leaving them out was the only way Roosevelt could gain the backing of "segregationist Southern Democrats in Congress," without whom nothing could have been done. But these reactionaries on the subject of race did not want to give collective bargaining rights to African-Americans, who, at the time, were employed largely in domestic and agricultural work. "President Roosevelt's compromise simply wrote workers in those industries out of the New Deal."

Since these workers were excluded from the laws offering

protection to labor, they were condemned to substandard conditions, ensuring that "poverty, brutal working conditions and legally sanctioned discrimination [would] persist for new generations of laborers, who are now mostly Latino immigrants."

The *Times* ends by noting that at long last New York fighters for labor's rights are pushing the passage of the Farmworkers Fair Labor Practices Act, "which would give these workers the rights that others have long taken for granted, as well as seek improvements in safety and sanitary conditions in the fields."

Source: *New York Times*, April 6, 2009 (editorial)

Comment: Isn't it strange that the people who harvest our food in the boiling sun are paid the least, treated the worst and disrespected the most, while the speculators in the Chicago futures markets who place bets on food prices are so much richer and work in air-conditioned offices? The New York legislation has passed the assembly, but expired in the Senate.

* * *

An earlier *New York Times* piece, cited in these pages, noted that pharmaceutical companies have recently seen fit to boost prices in preparation for possible changes in government healthcare programs. This next article, found in the *Wall Street Journal*, adds to this finding by underlining that hospitals, too, are getting into this game.

The article opens, "Hospital and pharmaceutical companies have been pushing through hefty price increases aimed at bolstering earnings, even as government and private insurers are struggling to rein in healthcare costs."

Figures from Credit Suisse show that this is the case with drugs such as Viagra and the leukemia pill Sprycel, both of which went up in price more than 20 percent since last year, which served to bolster their makers' bottom lines. Meanwhile, HCA Inc., a major hospital owner, is seeing revenue climb, even though it now has fewer hospitals in its stable and is recording fewer patients. This is a sure sign of boosted billings for those it continues to serve.

Credit Suisse's Catherine Arnold, who has been watching these trends, notes that these increases follow a common pattern of companies' actions in the face of policy changes. She stated, "When the government is talking about more aggressive discounts, your start price is going to determine your end price" and, so, firms find it to their advantage to ratchet up these start prices. Even so, this boosting is startlingly aggressive, as she comments, "I don't think I have ever seen anything quite like this."

Source: *Wall Street Journal*, April 15, 2009

Comment: The drug companies and hospital chains made sure that the health care reform law which passed in 2010 had no price controls or volume discounts. Uncle Sam is still prohibited from negotiating volume discounts for drugs bought with taxpayer money under the drug benefit program.

* * *

A shocking story coming out of West Virginia, by way of hard-hitting coverage in the *New York Times*, focuses on the cover-up of a plant explosion, which was justified under the excuse that releasing details would aid terrorists!

The tale began to unfold last August when, after a gigantic explosion "at a West Virginia chemical plant, managers refused for several hours to tell emergency responders the nature of the blast or the toxic chemical it released. They later misused a law intended to keep information from terrorists to try to stop federal investigators from learning what had happened, members of a House subcommittee said Tuesday."

As Matthew L. Wald writes, two workers were killed in the blast at the Bayer Crop-Science plant in Institute, West Virginia. Six volunteer firefighters were also made ill when they came in response to the emergency. The explosion was great enough to send a several-thousand-pound tank flying through the air, and to be felt at a 10 mile distance.

The investigation found that various actions had been taken, which, in the words of subcommittee chairman Representative Bart

Stupak, a Democrat of Michigan, made it look as if there were "an orchestrated effort by Bayer to shroud the explosion in secrecy." Suspicions were aroused by the fact that video cameras in the plant had been disconnected, and monitors used to detect releases of deadly chemical methyl isocyanate, "had been disabled."

While Congress created and authorized the Chemical Safety and Hazard Investigation Board to investigate just such disasters as these, Bayer's chief executive, William Buckner, "said in his prepared testimony that company officials believed they could 'refuse to provide information' to the Board." And, in a further attempt to keep information secret, the firm labeled a large mass of documents as containing "security-sensitive information," which, therefore, did not have to be revealed to the C.S.B.

As it turned out, "88 percent of the 2,000 documents it had marked as being 'security sensitive' were not."

In a stinging rebuke to the company, the chairman of the Energy and Commerce Committee, Henry Waxman, said, "I think it's finally time to ask whether it makes sense to allow Bayer to continue producing and storing such massive amounts" of toxic chemicals.

Source: *New York Times*, April 22, 2009 (by Matthew L. Wald)

In a *New York Times* article, Gardiner Harris writes about a study done by the Institute of Medicine, part of the National Academy of Science, which surveyed the relations between doctors and medical schools, on the one side, with pharmaceutical companies and medical device makers, on the other. The report came down hard on physicians who take "money, gifts and free drug samples" from these purveyors.

The report also made this point, "It is time for medical schools to end a number of long-accepted relationships and practices that create conflicts of interest, threaten the integrity of their missions and their reputations, and put public trust in jeopardy."

The situation is so harmful that the report is asking that Congress put into law the requirement that the companies selling drugs and devices disclose all monies and samples they give to doctors. A few legislators share the Institute's fears, with Senators Charles E. Grassley, Republican of Iowa, and Herb Kohl, Democrat of Wisconsin, pushing for a bill that would make company disclosure mandatory.

Such a law would touch upon a major area of drug company expenditure in that, as Harris noted, the billions the firms devote to doctors' perks, including samples, free meals and medical refresher courses, and fees to physicians for giving lectures, are "more than they spend on research or consumer advertising."

As to whether the Institute's recommendations will be heeded, Dr. P. Roy Vagelos, a former Merck chief executive, who has not been happy with companies lavishing so many gifts on doctors, stated, "I think medical centers and companies will start to listen to these recommendations and to take them very seriously."

Source: *New York Times*, April 29, 2009 (by Gardiner Harris)

Comment: The Grassley-Kohl bill is still languishing in the Senate.

* * *

A just-released report by the Government Accountability Office looked into Pentagon spending, giving special attention to the Missile Defense Agency, which since 2002 has run up bills of $56 billion, with $50 billion more on the horizon for the next five years.

This agency, according to the GAO whose report was covered in the *New York Times* by Christopher Drew, has cost overruns somewhere in the neighborhood of $2 billion to $3 billion.

As Drew noted, "The defense secretary, Robert M. Gates, has said he expects to propose cuts in some of the most troubled programs as part of an effort to remake a contracting system that has been plagued by cost overruns and delays."

And, even the huge estimated overruns for this one agency may not be accurate, the GAO admitted, because the Missile Defense Agency's "budgeting practices were not precise enough," and, so, their study of 2008 was the sixth in a row where the government auditors could not determine the real costs of the agency's programs.

Source: *New York Times*, March 18, 2009 (by Christopher Drew)

The number of defense contracting fraud and corporation cases sent by government investigators to prosecutors dropped precipitously under the Bush administration, even as contracting by the Defense Department almost doubled, the Center for Public Integrity reported last week.

Defense contracting grew from about $200 billion in fiscal year 1993 at the start of the Clinton presidency to nearly $400 billion in FY 2008 at the end of President George W. Bush's administration. (1993 dollars adjusted for inflation to 2008 dollars.)

But Defense Department investigators during the Bush administration sent 76 percent fewer contracting fraud and corruption cases to the Justice Department for potential criminal prosecution than were referred under Clinton, according to Justice Department data analyzed by the Center for Public Integrity.

"No one is minding the store," said William G. Dupree, a former director of the Defense Criminal Investigative Service (DCIS), which investigates contracting fraud. "Someone needs to address that."

[The] Defense Department Office of Inspector General's report to Congress in March 2008 states that investigation of contracting fraud is one area of many "that have dropped in priority and have largely been neglected." It is an area "in need of additional DCIS commitment." Defective pricing, cost and labor mischarging, product substitution, and other economic crimes, the report states, listing types of contracting fraud, "threaten DOD's financial well-being and endanger lives."

Source: *Corporate Crime Reporter*, April 6, 2009

"Recently, I went to a drugstore to fill a prescription," writes Tara Parker-Pope in the *New York Times*. "Instead, I left with a costly lesson in health care economics."

As she tells the story, "At the checkout, I was surprised when the clerk billed me for $100 instead of my usual small co-payment.

It was only then that I realized my doctor had traded me up to a costly branded migraine drug, even though the old drug had worked just fine. And I had allowed it."

Parker-Pope's message is that patients' inattention and doctors' lack of communication with those they are treating are factors to consider in looking into "the way medical care is delivered."

She cites a statement by an emergency medicine physician at St. Luke's Roosevelt Hospital Center in New York, Dr. David Newman, who also penned the eye-opening book *Hippocrates' Shadow: Secrets From the House of Medicine* (Simon and Schuster, 2008). As he sees it, "You can make policy changes till you're blue in the face, but if patients and doctors don't change that way they think about medicine, we'll never change medicine."

As has been suggested already in these pages, the U.S. has the unenviable position of paying more for its healthcare and getting fewer benefits than many other countries. As Parker-Pope explains, each year we spend $2.5 trillion on health care, which breaks down to about $8,160 per person. That's something like double what is budgeted in many countries in Europe, including those with universal coverage of their citizenry. In the U.S., by contrast, these high rates have to be paired with the fact that 46 million Americans have no insurance while, vis-à-vis the European countries, we are behind in maternal and childhood health as well as length of life. We are even behind many less-developed nations on these indices.

A glaring reason for the high-cost, low effectiveness of American medicine was underlined by another physician author, Dr. Marcia Angell, a senior lecturer in social medicine at Harvard Medical School, who wrote *The Truth About the Drug Companies: How They Deceive Us and What to Do About It* (Random House 2004). She states, "Doctors believe the industry propaganda that new drugs are better than old ones, and that for every ailment there is a drug. They learn to practice a drug-intensive style of medicine." And patients buy into the same mindset.

This can be graphically brought out by looking at the attitude of patients and doctors to 2002 government-financed clinical trials on pills to bring down high blood pressure. The study established that the generic pills worked better than the vastly pricier new pharmaceuticals. Yet, even after the results were made known, most hypertension patients are still being prescribed the heavily marketed, not only costlier, but less effective drugs pushed by the pharmaceutical companies.

Another example is that of ear infections. While it has repeatedly been shown these infections do not respond to antibiotics, doctors keep giving them. Often it is to treat a child at the parents' insistence. *The Archives of Internal Medicine* just published a study of this phenomenon that indicated 37 percent of doctors in a survey "complained that patients routinely demanded unnecessary prescriptions."

It's not only drugs that are often given needlessly but such procedures as medical scans or back surgery. And yet, an important 2004 study in *The American Journal of Public Health* brought out the interesting finding that "technology played a surprisingly minor role in improving health," especially compared with lifestyle changes such as losing weight and quitting smoking, plus public health measures such as the provision of clean water and inspected meat.

Newman summed up the situation in these words, "In American culture, prescriptions and procedures have become surrogates for real health care and real dialogue. We need doctors and patients to conceive of medicine and health in a totally different way than they have been taught in the last 20 to 30 years."

Source: *New York Times*, March 3, 2009 (by Tara Parker-Pope)

Many expected that after the taxpayers had bailed out the banks, these financial institutions would repay the favor by increasing lending. However, as David Gaffen put it in the *Wall Street Journal*, "Cash is king particularly at the nation's banking institutions."

It used to be, he notes, that banks kept about $300 billion on hand to tide them over in case of heavy withdrawals or for other unforeseen problems, but that has changed in the new financial ndscape. Banks seem to be have been shaken up by the fall of

Lehman Brothers Holdings and other collapses, and so have upped their holdings to generally above $1 trillion in assets.

Although that number may fluctuate, Gaffen writes, on Friday, the Federal Reserve recorded that for the week ending March 18, banks had a whopping $976 billion in cash on hand. It certainly appears these banks are being overly cautious in that the Federal Reserve is now both providing them with zero-cost borrowing and insuring them against risk through the Fed's liquidity programs. Even with these safeguards and profit opportunities, the banks are being stingy. Gaffen ends ruefully, "One would think that lending would have picked up a bit more."

Source: *Wall Street Journal*, March 31, 2009 (by David Gaffen)

Comment: One would think so! Especially since the banks turn around and charge twenty or more times the interest rate to small business and consumer borrowers.

* * *

Zachary A. Goldfarb reported in the *Washington Post* that Countrywide Financial was responsible for many of the ill-considered housing loans that, when they went sour in 2007, greatly weakened the company, which ended up being sold to Bank of America.

Goldfarb writes, "Executives at Countrywide Financial, one of the biggest names of the housing boom, routinely violated internal company policies to provide below-market rates on home loans to the politically connected and powerful, according to a congressional report to be released today."

The congress's review of loan documents revealed a special VIP program, dubbed "Friends of Angelo," after the firm's chief executive Angelo Mozilo, which funneled loans at low rates to the powerful. Among the recipients were top businessmen, journalists, celebrities, and government personnel, from congressional aides, all the way up to such luminaries as Senator Kent Conrad (D. ND), Senator Christopher J. Dodd (D. CT), former U.S. ambassador

Richard C. Holbrooke, former Fannie Mae chief executive James Johnson, and former Department of Housing and Urban Development secretary Alphonso Jackson.

According to Goldfarb, "Most recipients of VIP loans have said in news accounts that they had no idea they were receiving a special deal. But the report states that Countrywide 'clearly' indicated to borrowers they were getting special deals, usually by including business cards indicating the loan came from a VIP unit."

One employee, Robert Finberg, who worked on VIP loans, said anyone receiving such a good deal was told upfront, "Your loan was specially priced by Angelo."

Source: *Washington Post*, March 19, 2009 (by Zachary A. Goldfarb)

Comment: VIP discounts are a widespread practice by large corporations in their interactions with VIPs—a kind of pervasive bribery that needs more investigation.

* * *

Newly empowered by the Supreme Court, the attorneys general of several states hit hard by the housing collapse are exploring consumer fraud suits against major mortgage lenders.

Frustrated by the banks' inability or unwillingness to stop an avalanche of foreclosures, the states are considering lawsuits over the creation and marketing of millions of bad loans as well as the dismal pace of mortgage modifications.

Source: *New York Times*, November 3, 2009 (by David Streitfeld and John Collins Rudolf)

Another excellent piece in the *Washington Post* comes from Tomoeh Murakami Tse. It opens with what will seem quite a paradox to those not acquainted with the world of executive compensation. "FBR Capital Markets failed to reach its performance goals in 2008. But the board of the Arlington investment bank awarded six-figure payouts to its executives anyway."

The company explained what might be considered rewards for work not done by saying executives "perform functions that are not directly related to the corporate performance" of the firm. And FBR is hardly exceptional in the disconnect between companies doing poorly, something reflected in declining share prices, and their executives, who earn high salaries, even bonuses, in the face of these dreadful results.

To make it seem their executives deserve these tidy paychecks, the monies are passed off as "retention awards," payment for not leaving the company or, so the discrepancy isn't too great, performance goals are lowered.

The list of companies that dole out generous rewards to those whose companies are ailing run from New York Stock Exchange operator NYSE Euronext to Oregon tech firm FEI.

To return to FBR, which recently changed its name to Arlington Asset Investment, it has been in a significant down slide. Last year, it recorded a $195 million loss as its stock nosedived nearly 50 percent. Meanwhile, as noted above totally ignoring these results, the company let two executives pick up handsome bonuses.

Source: *Washington Post*, March 19, 2009 (by Tomoeh Murakami Tse)

Comment: Wouldn't workers be delighted to have the same deal for their pay, especially if they get to appoint their paymasters the way top bosses appoint, wine and dine their nicely paid board of directors?

* * *

Sharing the spotlight with the company mentioned in the last citation for granting inappropriate executives bonuses is American International Group.

A.I.G. is the insurance company that, when it was on the verge of collapse, was bailed out by the U.S. government with a handover of $200 billion, giving the feds an 80 percent stake in the firm. That's why many in Congress *got steamed* when it began handing out big checks to its executives.

However, this brazen company is not done yet in trying to take advantage of the government, as Lynnley Browning reports in the *New York Times*. She comments that A.I.G. "is quietly fighting the federal government for the return of $306 million in tax payments, some related to deals that were conducted through offshore tax havens."

How is this taking place? "A.I.G. sued the government last month in a bid to force it to return the payments, which stemmed in large part from A.I.G.'s use of aggressive tax deals, some involving entities controlled by the company's financial products unit in the Cayman Islands, Ireland, the Dutch Antilles and other offshore havens."

Ironically enough, in pursuing these refunds, A.I.G. is using some of the taxpayers' $200 billion, which is a legal action on its part.

Source: *New York Times*, March 20, 2009 (by Lynnley Browning)

Comment: Can you imagine any individual, no matter how rich, getting a huge taxpayer bailout and then suing to get a tax refund from the government that bailed the individual out? Corporate supremacy and corporate gall at work. And the executive bonuses still keep coming.

* * *

Along with banks and insurance companies, other key players in the recent financial downturn were credit-rating companies, which, as Serena Ng and Lis Rappaport write in the *Wall Street Journal*, have been "widely assailed for their role in fueling the financial crisis with overly rosy debt ratings." Even with their bad press, they are about to earn a billion dollars as part of a new government project to kick-start the weak credit markets.

The plan works like this. The government, through the Federal Reserve, is issuing a cool $7 billion in bonds. But no one is going to buy these bonds unless they get good marks from at least two of the three main credit rating firms, viz., Moody's Investors Service, Standard & Poor's Ratings Services and Fitch Ratings.

So, even though the three firms showed notable bad judgment in over-rating poor mortgage securities, the ones that dropped like rocks when the housing market plummeted, they are still the only game in town, and the government needs their imprimatur on its new issue.

The upshot is that "the government is in the uncomfortable position of rewarding these same firms" who lately failed miserably in assigning proper ratings. This time, though, if they make another mistake, it's not insurance companies and banks, but the government (and taxpayers) who will take the fall.

Source: *Wall Street Journal*, March 20, 2009 (by Serena Ng and Lis Rappaport)

Comment: Nothing succeeds like chronic failure by these corporations. Deterrence goes out the window.

* * *

New York Times science writer Gina Kolata described a medical case, which revealed some of the worst features of our current healthcare regime. As she begins, "When Gail Kislevitz had an M.R.I. scan of her knee, it came back blurry, 'uninterpretable,' her orthopedist told her.

"Her insurer refused to pay for another scan, but the doctor said he was sure she had torn cartilage that stabilizes the knee and suggested an operation to fix it. After the surgery, Ms. Kislevitz, 57, of Ridgewood, N.J. received a surprise: the cartilage had not been torn after all."

Although fortunately, she didn't have to pay for the procedures, which were covered by her insurer, she ended up with a long rehabilitation after which her sore knee was no better than when she started.

The key issue here is medical scanning. It's big business, with above 95 million high-tech scans carried out every year in the U.S. The price tag for these procedures is $100 billion a year, with only a limited $14 billion covered by Medicare. And studies have suggested that, just as in the case of the scan done on Ms. Kislevits, from 20 to 50 percent were unneeded.

Given that vast wastage, Dr. Vijay Rao, chairwoman of the radiology department at Thomas Jefferson University Hospital in Philadelphia, stated, "The system is just totally, totally broken."

One problem, again as in the case of Kislevits, is that many scans are botched and so reveal nothing about what they were intended to examine, and many who conduct the procedures are under-qualified. Though a patient may be medically savvy, he or she can do little about a scan except to ask for assurances that it is necessary and make sure the person performing the scan is accredited.

Moreover, even if the job is well done and called for, it's certainly a situation open to abuse since, as Kolata reports, a "growing number of doctors ... refer patients for imaging done by scanners they own and profit from. Studies have found that up to 3.2 times as many scans are ordered in such cases."

Dr. Bruce Hillman, a radiology professor at the University of Virginia, charges that all too often physicians are seduced by this easy money. He stated, "It's all profits" in that doctors who club together and purchase a scanner can add "an extra $500,000 to $1 million a year" to their income.

Source: *New York Times*, March 2, 2009 (by Gina Kolata)

A moment ago, we read a *New York Times* article about how A.I.G. was trying to squeeze even more money out of the government by fighting for a tax refund. A second article in the same paper goes on to note that all the money handed to the firm, "in loans, investments and equity injections, to keep it afloat," were hardly rewards for good behavior. Just the opposite was the case. Because its practices had been so careless, A.I.G. was bringing the whole global financial system to the brink of chaos. That's why the federal government felt it had to be buoyed up.

Seamus P. McMahon, a banking expert at Booz & Company, pointed to the rationale behind government reasoning. "If we let

A.I.G. fail," then a host of other key institutions, including big banks and insurers "will face their own capital and liquidity crisis, and we could have a domino effect."

Frank Partnoy, a law professor at the University of San Diego and a derivatives expert, adds the other piece, that about A.I.G.'s delinquency. "They were the worst of them all," Partnoy said. Equally condemning, Donn Vickerey of Gradient Analytics attributed A.I.G.'s failure to "extreme hubris, fueled by greed."

The *Times* writer, Joe Nocera, closed on these somber words, "Other firms used many of the same shady techniques as A.I.G. but none did them on such a broad scale and with such utter recklessness. And yet—and this is the part that should make your blood boil—the company is being kept alive precisely because it behaved so badly."

Source: *New York Times*, February 28, 2009 (by Joe Nocera)

Comment: This is what too-big-to-fail looks like. This is what de-regulation run amok looks like. This is what Uncle Sam the Sucker looks like since A.I.G. makes many of its deals in foreign countries. Why didn't other countries like the UK, France, Germany and others share in the bailout? This is what corporate globalization looks like—a gigantic escape hatch from U.S. jurisdiction and its laws. This is what utterly powerless taxpayers look like until they organize big time. If they don't, it will happen again and again, because these giant companies hold the U.S. government and its taxpayers hostage. Meanwhile A.I.G. executives got bonuses after the collapse and bailout! Also about $70 billion in U.S. bailout money and guarantees went to foreign banks operating in the U.S.

* * *

"'I find it impossible to understand why we as taxpayers are bailing out foreign banks,' said Thomas H. Patrick, a founder of new Vernon Capital and a former top executive at Merrill Lynch. 'If the shoe was on the other foot and major U.S. institutions were exposed to those banks, would the U.K. or the E.U. tax their citizens to pay off JP Morgan? There has to be some explanation of why we decided to do that.'

"The top three recipients of money from the government related to the credit insurance A.I.G. had written are Societe Generale, a French bank, at \$11 billion; Goldman Sachs at \$8.1 billion; and Deustche Bank, at \$5.4 billion."

Not only are some financial experts irritated by the way the U.S. government is doling out money to foreign financial institutions, this *Times* report continues, they also are not happy with the fact that it took A.I.G. six months to supply the names of where its money was going.

Sylvain R. Raynes, founder of R& R Consulting, a company that helps customers study debt risks, feels that the delay suggests that the government was purposely misleading the public by "asking the American people, under the veil of secrecy, to bail out one company when, in fact, they wanted to bail out someone else." The subterfuge was prompted, Raynes feels, by the fact that the public would have clamored for their representatives to cancel the deal if they knew the whole story.

Source: *New York Times*, March 18, 2009 (by Gretchen Morgenson)

Comment: Much of what the Treasury Department did was of dubious legality. In a long profile on Henry Paulson, Bush's Treasury Secretary, Mr. Paulson admitted that he "didn't have the authorities" to make many decisions but he did it anyway because someone had to do it. (*Washington Post*, November 19, 2008)

* * *

An important piece by Cindy Skrzycki in the *Washington Post* calls attention to an underhanded ploy by the Bush administration in last fall passing an important bill concerning nursing homes "with no public notice or attention."

The outcome of the new regulation was to "shut off a source of information ... about abuse and neglect in long-term care facilities that people suing nursing homes consider crucial to their cases."

"This is pretty stunning," said Mark Kosieradzki, a plaintiff attorney in Plymouth, Minn. "Nobody was told. It was just done."

The law, which covers about 16,000 nursing facilities and their 3 million residents, reclassifies state inspectors as well as Medicare and Medicaid personnel as federal employees. This might seem a cosmetic change until it is realized that such federal employees generally do not have to provide evidence in court cases that touch on areas in which they work. Thus, people suing a nursing home will have to do a lot more work now to obtain depositions from them or to get access to their records than they had to do in the past.

Eric M. Carlson, an attorney with the National Senior Citizens Law Center in Los Angeles, noted the ramifications, "Government inspectors have the right to go into nursing homes and investigate, and they learn things that residents and families otherwise could never find out." This new, unheralded law puts a whole host of barriers in front of anyone who wanted to obtain information from these government records. Carlson states forthrightly, "This change hurts nursing-home residents and their families by allowing bad practices to be kept in secret by nursing homes and inspectors."

The Bush administration defended its rule change by saying that when these employees were asked to help in court cases, it took time away from them doing their duties of inspecting, certifying and enforcing the law in nursing homes.

The law's outcome is already evident in that information concerning nursing homes, which had been provided as a matter of course, is now "stalled between state and federal officials."

Source: *Washington Post*, February 24, 2009 (by Cindy Skrzycki)

Comment: The Bush directive has not been repealed by the Obama Administration, and is just one of many Bush rules that have not been rolled back by the victorious Democrats controlling both the Congress and the White House in 2009.

* * *

Another largely unheralded change, not in the law but in the economy, came about in 2004 when Bristol-Meyers Squibb decided to close the last U.S. plant that made a number of important ingredients for such antibiotics as penicillin. At the time, no one saw this as posing any danger to our nation's well being.

"But now," as Gardiner Harris writes in the *New York Times*, "experts and lawmakers are growing more and more concerned that the nation is far too reliant on medicine from abroad, and they are calling for a law that would require that certain drugs be made or stockpiled in the United States."

One outstanding proponent of this view is Senator Sherrod Brown, a Democrat of Ohio, who stated, "The lack of regulation around outsourcing is a blind spot that leaves room for supply disruptions, counterfeit medicines, even bio-terrorism."

Harris goes on to supply some crucial background to this issue. U.S. drug manufacturers, which not so long ago had all their plants in this country, have followed so many industries in moving abroad in search of cheaper labor in havens where there are fewer environmental and other regulations on business.

Following this massive offshore move, nowadays the key ingredients for almost all antibiotics as well as for a host of other pharmaceutical products, such as "the popular allergy medicine prednisone; metformin, for diabetes; and amlodipine, for high blood pressure," can only be obtained from China or India.

This can be seen in dramatic form by scanning over the manufacturing plants that are referred to in all the applications for permission to make generic drugs that were filed with the Food and Drug Administration in 2007. Of the 1,154 pharmaceutical factories that come up, a bare 13 percent were in the U.S. while the lion's share were either in China, with 43 percent, or India, with 39 percent.

Evidence of the foreign manufacture of many medicines is often concealed both because pharmaceutical companies will hide these sources as one of their trade secrets and because they will label their bottles with the name of the U.S. factory where final assembly, putting drug powders into pill casings, is done on ingredients made abroad.

Bear in mind that "some of these medicines are lifesaving, and health care in the United States depends on them. Half of all Americans take a prescription medicine every day."

Joe Acker, president of the Synthetic Organic Chemical Manufacturers Association, says that this imbalance is understandable, given that foreign plants can sidestep most of the regulations that are in force here. As he puts it, "U.S. companies are more regulated and are under more scrutiny than foreign producers, particularly those from emerging countries." As he sees it, "That's just totally backwards. We need a level playing field."

Equally of concern, though, is the threat posed by the foreign manufacture of key drugs abroad in the case of an epidemic. If a large-scale outbreak of a transmissible disease occurred, "the United States would not be able to rely on vaccines manufactured largely in Europe because of possible border closures and supply shortages."

Even without an epidemic, another blockage of the supply of crucial drugs might occur if the U.S. got into a trade dispute or other battle with China. As Dr. Yusef K. Hamied, chairman of Cipla, an Indian company that makes many pharmaceutical ingredients, expressed the danger of such extreme dependency on foreign suppliers. "If tomorrow China stopped supplying pharmaceutical ingredients, the worldwide pharmaceutical industry would collapse."

Enrico Polastro, a Belgian drug industry consultant, sees it like this, "If China ever got very upset with President Obama, it could be a big problem."

Source: *New York Times*, January 20, 2009, (by Gardiner Harris)

Comment: Chinese-made ingredients contaminated the drug Heparin, an anti-clotting medicine needed for surgery, causing at least 81 deaths plus hundreds of injuries in the U.S.

* * *

A new audit done jointly by the Special Inspector General for Iraq Reconstruction and the State Department's Inspector General has discovered that the company previously known as Blackwater Worldwide was overpaid by tens of millions of dollars for its work in Iraq, in which it did not supply as many personnel as it promised.

Where the firm had been hired to provide manpower to protect high-ranking officials, such as the U.S. ambassador, it was found not to have come up with a sufficient number of medics, security guards, dog handlers, and marksmen.

According to the audit, which was reported by Yochi J. Dreazen in the *Wall Street Journal*, "The failure to consistently field the right numbers of guards endangered the U.S. officials whom the company was being paid to protect." Furthermore, it concluded. "Insufficient manning exposed the department to unnecessary risk."

Blackwater closed up shop in Iraq earlier in 2009 because the Iraqi government wanted the company out after it was involved in a 2007 incident where one of its security teams was embroiled in a fight that killed 17 Iraqis. Five former Blackwater employees, who were involved in that shooting, have been charged by the U.S. with manslaughter. The company has also been sued over this action by a number of Iraqi families whose members died in the incident.

The audit is just the latest scandal to swirl around Blackwater, "which was for years the best known Western contractor in Iraq." It doesn't come at a good time for the company, which, under its new name Xe, is trying to land new contracts for the war in Afghanistan. It is angling for tens of millions of dollars in business supplying such services as "training Afghan personnel to flying cargo for the U.S. military."

Source: *Wall Street Journal*, June 16, 2009 (by Yochi J. Dreazen)

Comment: Astonishingly, Blackwater, now Xe, did receive contracts including one for $120 million to guard some U.S. consulates in Afghanistan, notwithstanding its criminal behavior and gouging of the taxpayers. Perhaps, Blackwater, having performed sensitive military functions for the U.S. Army, knows too much. Perhaps, this is some of what President Dwight Eisenhower, warned about in his farewell address (1960) regarding what he famously called "the military-industrial complex."

* * *

Another recently issued government report is profiled by the *Wall Street Journal,* this time in an astute piece by Leslie Scism. The government study damns the "Treasury Department for allowing life insurers to buy tiny savings and loans to qualify for bailout funds," in a way that may be technically legal but certainly breaks with the "spirit" of the Troubled Asset Relief Program, the government venture that sought to increase spending by banks in the wake of the financial meltdown.

The report by the special inspector general examined the behavior of Hartford Financial Services Group Inc. and Lincoln National Corporation, both of whom had acquired small banks and, subsequently, between them, took $4.35 billion in TARP money. Where the money was supposed to be spent in relation to the newly acquired banks, instead, the report learned, those funds were used to buy bonds that could be used to back the insurance companies, which then allowed them "to issue additional annuities and life insurance."

As the report made plain, with this strategy of buying the "tiny thrifts," the firms, which in their mainstay insurance business have little concern with consumer lending, "gained access to more than $4.3 billion in taxpayer funds, an amount that is many multiples of the thrifts' total assets."

Source: *Wall Street Journal,* December 11, 2009 (by Leslie Scism)

As David Streitfeld, writing in the *New York Times,* points out, "Mortgage rates in the United States have dropped to their lowest levels since the 1940s, thanks to a trillion-dollar intervention by the federal government. Yet the banks that once handed out home loans freely are imposing such stringent requirements that many homeowners who might want to refinance are effectively locked out."

He notes, further, that these restrictions couldn't come at a worse time since at the moment there seems to be a small uptick in employment and consumer spending, which could be partially derailed by the paucity of available mortgage credit.

If home owners were now able to refinance, they could free up "hundreds of dollars a month," money that could then be employed in new spending or debt repayment. This new money put into circulation could further buoy the economy. And that's not counting the fact that refinancing might help some people whose homes are in jeopardy because they can't afford high mortgage payments, but could keep paying if these rates were adjusted downward.

Source: *New York Times*, December 13, 2009 (by David Streitfeld)

Comment: Again, do you think that an individual, no matter how rich, could have pulled off what these corporations took for themselves? Is this another example of a double standard between real human beings and the artificial entity called a corporation?

* * *

A *New York Times* editorial, entitled "Trust, Antitrust and Your Vote" discusses the danger imposed by a coming near monopolization of the voting machine industry by one company. It was prompted by the fact that our country's biggest manufacturer of voting machines, Election Systems and Software, announced it is purchasing the U.S. voting machine division of Diebold, its largest rival. That puts it in control of "nearly 70 percent of the nation's voting precincts... and raises serious antitrust questions and serious concerns about the vulnerability of future elections."

Not only would this near monopoly cause the usual problems that occur when a firm is not reined in from exploiting its customers by competitors, but it means that if problems arose, anything from an accidental failure of the system to sabotage, "it could have a disastrous effect on the entire nation's vote."

The *Times* editorialist mentioned that this planned purchase has not gone unnoticed by others, including voting-rights groups, and Senator Charles Schumer, who has asked the Attorney General to carefully investigate the deal from the antitrust angle.

A smaller voting machine producer, Hart InterCivic, which has placed its machines in about 9 percent of U.S. precincts, has already gone to court in Delaware to dispute the sale, saying the establishment of this new, mega-company "could harm the company's [Hart's] ability to retain customers and attract new ones."

The *Times* recommends "the Justice Department and state attorneys general" should also become party to this lawsuit on the side of Hart, presenting the argument that the combined voting machine company "would make the voting experience worse and reduce the reliability of election results." The editorial also calls on Justice's antitrust division to stop the sale if possible.

Given that the 2000 presidential election was filled with disputes over voting machines, this is a touchy subject with the public. Therefore, the piece ends, "we fear that if any one voting machine maker is allowed to dominate the market, there will be even greater reasons to worry about the nation's flawed voting system."

Source: *New York Times*, October 28, 2009 (editorial)

Wendell Potter tells the following story.

I'm the former insurance industry insider now speaking out about how big for-profit insurers have hijacked our health care system and turned it into a giant ATM for Wall Street investors, and how the industry is using its massive wealth and influence to determine what is (and is not) included in the health care reform legislation members of Congress are now writing.

I thought I could live with being a well-paid huckster and hang in there a few more years until I could retire.

While visiting my folks in northeast Tennessee where I grew up, I read in the local paper about a health "expedition" being held that weekend a few miles up U.S. 23 in Wise, VA. Doctors, nurses and other medical professionals were volunteering there to provide free medical care to people who lived in the area. What intrigued me most was that Remote Area Medical, a non-profit group whose original mission was to provide free care to people in remote villages in South America, was organizing the expedition. I decided to check it out.

The 50-mile stretch of U.S. 23, which twists through the mountains where thousands of men have made their living working in the coalmines turned out to be my "road to Damascus."

Nothing could have prepared me for what I saw when I reached the Wise County Fairgrounds, where the expedition was being held. Hundreds of people had camped out all night in the parking lot to be assured of seeing a doctor or dentist when the gates opened. By the time I got there, long lines of people stretched from every animal stall and tent where the volunteers were treating patients.

That scene was so visually and emotionally stunning it was all I could do to hold back tears. How could it be that citizens of the richest nation in the world were being treated this way?

A couple of weeks later I was boarding a corporate jet to fly from Philadelphia to a meeting in Connecticut. When the flight attendant served my lunch on gold-rimmed china and gave me a gold-plated knife and fork to eat it with, I realized for the first time that someone's insurance premiums were paying for me to travel in such luxury. I also realized that one of the reasons those people in Wise County had to wait in long lines to be treated in animal stalls was because our Wall Street-driven health care system has created one of the most inequitable health care systems on the planet.

I quit my job last year.

Source: Wendell Potter, formerly vice-president for Cigna, and author of *Deadly Spin: An Insurance Company Insider Speaks Out on How Corporate PR Is Killing Health Care and Deceiving Americans,* speaking on June 24, 2009 at the Center for Media and Democracy

AFTERMATH
Are you Ready for the Action

Well, here you are with fresh memories of what you have just read. Pretty rotten abuses aye? But, we've got the power to stop these big corporations from running the country into the ground.

Getting Steamed produces fact-driven emotional indignation. Without the proverbial "fire in the belly," even the informed mind remains in its routines; nothing happens. With it, you can think about the next stages, well expressed back in 14th Century China when a philosopher declared "To Know and Not to Do is Not to Know!"

One can be quite self-contained and calm yet express oneself about these business abuses and their limitless greed and cruelty with words like:

"These people should be jailed!"

"What they did was just awful."

"These companies have no self-restraint."

"Corporate crime pays—until it doesn't."

"Amazing how resourcefully clever they are—just to think up these schemes, these tricks that take advantage of us. Disgusting, really."

"They're just out of control."

"Where are the prosecutors? The lawmakers? It looks like the fat cats have rigged the whole system in their favor."

"The little guy doesn't have a chance and that's a damn shame."

"What can we do about all this—it just seems to be getting worse and unstoppable? Even after the Wall Street crash and Washington bailout, it is still business as usual."

"Sure I'm mad, but I'm just one person, what can I do?"

"Small business would never get away with this stuff."

"These crooks make a mockery of the free market."

What *can* be done about all this unbridled greed? Would you more likely start doing something if you knew that 1,000 other Americans connected with one another including you, also wanted to do something about corporate crime? How about 10,000, 100,000 or even 1,000,000 people agreeing to get something underway to rescue our country and its workers, its citizens, its families, its children, its environment from these rapacious exploiters of health, safety and economic well-being?

By now, you may be asking—ok, what is that something? Let's start at what can be called a critical mass of organized Americans to deal with widespread corporate abuses in a systematic way, including fostering deterrence to prevent future wrongdoing. I am referring to one million Americans getting together for collective action, from various backgrounds, well distributed geographically in all 435 *Congressional Districts* through fifty states. Let's imagine these people each signs on to raise or contribute $100 a year and dedicate 100 volunteer hours to push our Senators and Representatives to deal with corporate crime. The goal: Enacting a comprehensive law and order reform agenda designed to make corporations subordinated to both our Constitution and the sovereignty of the people. When they harm people with their fraudulent commercial assaults or inflict harmful side-effects on innocent people and their environments, these perpetrators would be brought to justice whether by effective law enforcement or civil actions. Think how much the American people will save in money and anguish if these corporate outrages are stopped in the future.

It will take a strong level of civic-political commitment to establish action offices with staff in each Congressional district, a cluster of backup centers and clearinghouses for close, fast coordination to get corrective legislation through our 535 lawmakers. Many of these measures are very long overdue. Already well-developed are many innovative ways to not only make these companies and their executives take responsibility for their actions but also to empower people so, when they are harmed, they are able to defend themselves and hold their perpetrators solidly accountable. Doing so will deter future misconduct.

Corporate reform should consist of two major principles

and several specific forms of law and order. The principles are *subordination* of corporate power to the *sovereignty* of the people as befits both the preamble to the Constitution—"We the People"—and the absence of any reference to corporations or companies in the text. The second principle is increasing *displacement* of the enormous corporate economy by *community* economics including more credit unions, local food markets, local renewable and efficient energy sources, community health clinics, community broadband, participatory community sports and recreational activities.

The goal of corporate law and order requires the following:

1. Larger law enforcement budgets for smarter law enforcement and sanctions that will pay for themselves many times over just in fines and disgorgements.
2. Broader facilities for workers, consumers and taxpayers to band together and usable rights to access the courts and regulatory agencies for their grievances. To shift power to the people who pay all the bills.
3. Real powers for investor-shareholders, the owners of corporations, to control their hired corporate hands who think they can mismanage and plunder the corporate treasuries for their own staggering enrichment.
4. Effective protections for whistleblowers who expose wrongdoing to the authorities, the media or civic groups.
5. More flexible regulatory options to avert the endless delays that corporate attorneys can inflict on any agency proceedings that enforces the law against violations and issues strong, updated health, safety and economic honesty standards.
6. Revive the antitrust laws to break up cartels, monopolies, oligopolies, and giant multinationals that are deemed "too big to fail, tax, or punish."
7. Establish accessible procedures for states to revoke or suspend corporate charters when companies exhibit harmful behavior. Install provisions for environmental bankruptcies, for example, with replacement of the officers

and boards of directors by trustees whose mission is to stop and repair severe damage to public health and natural resources and reorganize the company's environental behavior.

8. End corporate personhood to make this artificial entity unequal and accountable to real human beings, under constitutions and statutes.

9. Enact federal charters for larger corporations to establish a new social compact, between them and the people, that facilitates many of the afore-mentioned reforms. "National charters for national corporations" were supported a century ago by presidents Theodore Roosevelt, William Howard-Taft and Woodrow Wilson.

There is a broad consensus in our country… The People do not want a repeat performance by crooks and speculators who enrich themselves using other people's money and then take their greedy recklessness to Washington to demand the taxpayers save them so that they can do it again and again.

And to reiterate, our bottom line is that corporations must be our servants not our masters.

Whatever motivates us to act together, such as recalling the best triumphs from our country's history by ordinary people together achieving extraordinary changes, will help. So, too, will the serious rising trends of rampaging corporate power and immunity reported in the previous pages. But nothing should energize us more than actively adopting the role of alert trustees for our children and their children, and making sure the country we bequeath to them is in better shape because of *what we do now for their future*. When we fight for their justice, and their freedom, we advance a deeper, fairer democracy. See pledge next page.

Are you rightfully steamed? If so, please check at which of four levels of serious mutual commitment, you will give or raise $100 (or more if you wish) a year and devote 100 (or more if you wish) volunteer hours a year. Invite your own circle of friends, neighbors and co-workers to join you in pledging. Call them your "little republics" to start the drive with us for national recovery and transformation.

Yes, I pledge to contribute at least $100 and 100 volunteer hours for coordinated, fundamental corporate reforms and self-initiatory powers for the people to protect themselves, when I am directly informed to my satisfaction that:

☐   999 other Americans sign the same pledge (the pioneers)
☐   9,999 other Americans sign the same pledge (the founders)
☐   99,999 other Americans sign the same pledge (the drivers)
☐ 999,999 other Americans sign the same pledge (the critical
       massers)

_____

Signature

_____

Name (please print)

_____

Street

_____

City, State, Zip

email address_____

Please send a copy of this pledge form to:
Center for Study of Responsive Law
P.O. Box 19367
Washington, DC 20036

In the meantime, I immediately want to learn more about corporate control, its history, and the changes needed for securing more productive, safe and responsible business behaviors in our country. I am enclosing $30 to receive both the ground-breaking hardback book *The People's Business* by Lee Drutman and Charlie Cray (with a Foreword by Ralph Nader) and the practical handbook *Taking on the Corporation* by Professor Emeritus Ralph Estes.

Please make checks payable to:
Center for Study of Responsive Law
P.O. Box 19367
Washington, DC 20036

To pay for the books or to make a donation online visit:
www.csrl.org/steamed/

Index